COLLEGE
FINANCIAL AID

How To Get Your <u>FAIR SHARE</u>

Peter V. Laurenzo, CFP®

College Financial Aid: How To Get Your Fair Share

©2010 by Peter V. Laurenzo,CFP®

Hudson Financial Press
College Aid Planning Associates, Inc.

4 Executive Park Drive

Albany, New York, 12203

Cataloging-in-Publication Data

Laurenzo, Peter V.
College Financial Aid: How To Get Your Fair Share/
Peter V. Laurenzo

8th Edition

ISBN 978-0-9629961-7-7
378.30973 — dc20

1. Student aid — United States —
   Handbooks, manuals, etc.
2. Scholarships
3. Student loan funds

This book is dedicated to the parents. You have nurtured your children through elementary, middle school and high school, and now you have one more educational hurdle in front of you. Seeing your son or daughter leaving home and going to college will be as surreal of an experience as the school's price tag. Hopefully the material in this book will make it a little easier for you. The good news is that most parent's will survive this venture.

About The Author

Peter V. Laurenzo is President of College Aid Planning Associates, Inc. based in Albany, New York. He has a Master's Degree in Education, is a Certified Financial Planner™, is a member of the Financial Planning Association and President of the National Financial Aid Practitioners Alliance. In addition to maintaining his full-time financial planning practice, Mr. Laurenzo presents financial aid seminars at schools and to employee groups throughout New York State, has written and taught financial aid courses nationally for other financial planners, and has been a guest on radio and television.

TABLE OF CONTENTS

CHAPTER FIVE
FEDERAL AID PROGRAMS

CHAPTER SIX
IN SEARCH OF MORE MONEY

CHAPTER SEVEN
EDUCATION TAX INCENTIVES

APPENDIX

INTRODUCTION

Most families lack the knowledge that will ensure their children will qualify for as much financial aid as they are legally entitled to. This lack of understanding is not only costly, but it often prohibits a student from attending the school of choice. Financial aid is not a gimmick; it is a system of rules, formulas, strategies and compromises. If you don't understand the system, you will inevitably pay more than the person who does.

It is evident that families lose thousands of dollars of financial aid each year because they are uninformed or misinformed about the financial aid process. Many families who didn't qualify for any aid would have received aid with proper planning. Do all families qualify for financial aid other than federal loans? Of course not. There are many factors that determine how much a family is entitled to receive. Do not assume ineligibility without first investigating the facts!

Most families do not have adequate funds accumulated to pay for a four-year college education. There is an abundance of statistical information illustrating how much you should be saving on a monthly basis to accumulate the amount of money you will need by the time your children reach college age. The reality is that most people don't have the disposable income available to accomplish this goal. Save as much as you can for your children's education, but be sure you don't compromise their aid eligibility by saving in the wrong places.

What I am going to present to you are sound financial aid planning principles to help you strategically plan for receiving your fair share of college financial aid. By utilizing this concise and non-technical format, parents and students will be able to understand, conceptualize and be pro-active throughout this often very confusing process.

This book will be an asset to families with students in college, students on the threshold of college and for families with young children who want to effectively plan for college. This information is critical whether you have no savings and need to know where the money will come from, or if you have accumulated savings and want to stretch it out as far as possible. Finally, this information should be coordinated with your investment advisor. Your financial objectives may be severely compromised if strategic planning for financial aid is not incorporated into a college savings program.

NOTICE: *Unless specifically indicated, the information in this text is focused on dependent students. Although there is a commonality of financial aid principles with dependent and independent status, percentages, assessments and regulations may differ.*

FACT OR FICTION

Myth   There is little financial aid available.

On the contrary, the Federal government alone has committed over $100 billion towards the cost of higher education. This, in addition to state aid programs and individual college aid programs, constitutes an enormous resource, if you know how to pursue it.

Myth   You have to be poor to receive financial aid.

There are many families with incomes over $100,000 that receive significant need-based aid, particularly at private colleges. Income is only one component of need analysis.

Myth   There is no way to change the amount of aid you may be eligible for.

College financial aid is not a black and white process. This book will demonstrate how to effectively prepare you for financial aid. The employment of some basic planning techniques can result in an increase in financial aid from a few hundred to thousands of dollars each year.

Myth   The way to find money is to search for scholarships.

Unfortunately too much effort is often dedicated to this pursuit. The vast majority of financial assistance will come from need-based financial aid and/or merit aid from the college the student attends. For more information on this myth, read the section on Scholarship Search Services.

Myth   If your son or daughter moves or is ejected out of the house, they will be able to file as an independent.

It's not quite that easy! There are specific criteria for establishing independent status. Carefully read the section on Dependent Versus Independent.

Myth   If we don't qualify for student aid, I'll have my child take out student loans.

Federal Student Loans have specific borrowing limits. In most cases, the amount a student can borrow through federal programs will not be enough to pay all college expenses.

GETTING ACQUAINTED
WITH THE SYSTEM

AN OVERVIEW OF FINANCIAL AID

A financial aid form must be completed to determine eligibility for federal and institutional funding. All students applying for financial aid must complete the Free Application For Federal Student Aid (FAFSA). This application qualifies students for Federal student aid programs, is used to qualify the student for institutional aid at certain colleges, and is often linked to the student's state education department for state aid programs. A student cannot receive a federal student loan without completing this application. In addition to the FAFSA, many colleges and universities also require The College Board Financial Aid Profile application. This additional and more comprehensive form further qualifies the student for institutional aid, as well as providing the financial aid officer with room to make professional judgment decisions regarding the student's need. Keep in mind that the admission process is a separate entity to the financial aid process.

The FAFSA is sent to a Federal processing center and the information is entered into the Federal Need Analysis Formula. This data is used to calculate the student's Expected Family Contribution (EFC) for Federal aid. The Expected Family Contribution is how much the family should be responsible to pay for college, before Federal aid eligibility commences. It is not necessarily what the family will pay. This EFC (often in conjunction with Profile) is also used as a benchmark by many schools for determining how much institutional aid the student may be eligible for.

The financial aid forms require information concerning student income and assets, parental income and assets, number of family members attending school, family size, and many other questions, which are weighted in determining your Expected Family Contribution. Many applicants find the form intimidating and confusing. If you do, get help. It is frightening to recall the number of people who did not complete the forms because of their frustration with them. If you do not submit a financial aid form, you will not be considered for financial aid! Statistics published of families who do not file for financial aid and who would be eligible for aid is alarming.

After admission acceptance, the financial aid department from each respective school will send the student an award letter. This is an itemized list of the kinds and amounts of financial aid that is being offered to the student. If the aid package is acceptable, it is signed and returned to the college. With the exception of completing loan applications, this basically concludes the process for that academic year. Each year, the process starts over with new forms and potentially new aid packages.

"And I have orthodontic bills, and my property
taxes increased and..."

COLLEGE COST

MINUS

EXPECTED FAMILY
CONTRIBUTION

EQUALS

DEMONSTRATED FINANCIAL
NEED

EXPECTED FAMILY CONTRIBUTION

A critical component of the financial aid equation is the student's Expected Family Contribution (EFC). The EFC is the sum of the parents' contribution and the student's contribution. The EFC, minus the total cost of the school (cost of attendance), is the amount of need you are demonstrating, and therefore the amount of aid you are eligible for. For financial aid purposes, a budget (total cost of the school) is established by each individual school. The budgeted costs will include tuition, room and board, books, miscellaneous fees, personal expenses, and a travel allowance. If the cost of attendance is more than the EFC, you have demonstrated need. If the cost of attendance is less than the EFC, you are not demonstrating need and are therefore ineligible for need-based federal financial aid. Keep in mind that federal student loans are available to students who do not demonstrate need, if they complete a FAFSA. Although a student may not have federal need, he or she may still have state aid eligibility.

A student applies to a school with a total cost of $25,000 and has a $15,000 Expected Family Contribution. That student has demonstrated $10,000 of need, and therefore is eligible for $10,000 of aid. That student also applies to a school with a total cost of $8,000. Since the Expected Family Contribution is $15,000, need has not been demonstrated.

AID COMES FROM

FEDERAL
➡ GRANTS
➡ LOANS
➡ WORK-STUDY

STATE
➡ GRANTS

COLLEGE
➡ GRANTS
➡ MERIT AID
➡ COLLEGE JOB SERVICE

WHERE FINANCIAL AID COMES FROM

Financial aid flows from three primary sources:

Federal Aid: Federal aid can include grants, loans and/or work-study programs.

State Aid: Many states have aid programs, which may include grants and loans, as well as special subsidies. Since state aid programs vary, you should check with the appropriate agency in your state. Generally, state aid is not available for nonresidents.

Institutional Aid: Grants and need-based scholarships constitute the majority of institutional (college) aid. Scholarships based solely on merit (academic or sports) are not determined by need, but often will impact the student's need-based aid package.

The maximum amount of federal and state aid available will often be insufficient to offset demonstrated need. It is the decision of the college to determine how much of that deficit will be made up with their own funds. Some schools will meet that deficit totally, thus the percent of need met would be 100%. Some schools will offer no gift aid while some schools will offer partial gift aid. "Gapping" occurs when a financial aid package meets less than 100% of the student's demonstrated need. There has been a significant increase in schools that have been unable or unwilling to meet 100% of need in the past few years. It is no secret that some schools are reaping larger endowments and grants than others; thus more funds can be allocated to students in need. In addition, with a steady increase in student population, institutional funds are being diluted.

It is important to remember that the financial aid process, like filing income taxes, occurs every year the student wants to be considered for aid. If there are dramatic changes in a family's financial or personal situation in any given year, it is likely that the subsequent aid packages will reflect those changes.

Students are notified of the type of aid package the school is offering in the form of an award letter. The award letter breaks down the aid for the following school year. The composition or makeup of the aid being offered should be scrutinized. Financial aid can be classified into two categories: Self-help and gift aid. Self-help includes loans and work-study programs while gift aid is comprised of grants and scholarships. You may have two like-priced schools and be offered the same dollar amount of aid, but the aid packages may be totally different. One school may be heavily weighted in the self-help area, whereas the other school may offer more gift aid. Obviously, the latter is a more desirous package, since gift aid does not have to be repaid. By applying to more than one school, you will have the opportunity to "shop" the financial aid packages.

A student has an Expected Family Contribution of $10,000 and the student applies to two schools with identical costs ($25,000). Both schools offer an aid package of $15,000 (the difference between EFC and the college's budgeted cost of $25,000). School A offers $5,500 in loans, $1,500 of Work-Study and an $8,000 institutional grant. School B's package was comprised of a $5,500 loan, and a $9,500 institutional grant. Although both schools met 100% of the demonstrated need, School B offered a better aid package because it had a higher percentage of gift aid. In today's world, either one of these packages would be an excellent offer!

RECAPPING THE PROCESS

☐   The student and/or parents complete the Free Application for Federal Student Aid (FAFSA) and CSS Profile, if required.

☐   The FAFSA is electronically sent to a Federal need analysis processing center.

☐   A Student Aid Report (SAR) is generated and mailed back to the student; a facsimile of that report is transmitted to the school(s) listed on the financial aid form.

☐   After the student has been accepted at a school, the school sends an Award Letter to the student, notifying him or her of the financial aid package being offered.

AID SEQUENCE

FREE APPLICATION FOR
FEDERAL STUDENT AID
⇩
NEED ANALYSIS PROCESSOR
⇩
STUDENT AID REPORT
⇩
AWARD LETTER

Don't Assume Ineligibility!

I cannot overstate the importance of filing for financial aid.

I recall a meeting with a couple who had two children in college. Jason, a sophomore, was attending a school with a price tag of $20,000, while Jennifer, a junior, was enrolled in a $16,000 college. Prior to our meeting, they had never completed a financial aid form. Since their combined income was nearly $80,000 and they owned a fair amount of assets, they assumed they were ineligible for aid. After perusing the financial aid forms, they decided completing them would just be a waste of time. Upon reviewing their income and assets, and inputting the necessary information into a Federal need analysis calculator, we arrived at an Expected Family Contribution of $7,500 per child. This means, if they had completed the financial aid forms, Jason would have been eligible for $12,500 of aid, while Jennifer would have been eligible for $8,500. $21,000 errors happen too frequently. As stated previously, a student cannot receive a federal loan if the FAFSA is not completed. In addition, many states link the FAFSA to their state aid programs. A student may be ineligible for federal aid or institutional aid other than loans, but may have state aid eligibility

"Student assets — that'll be 20% please."

CHAPTER
TWO

FINANCIAL AID PLANNING STRATEGIES

Student Assets

The impact of student assets in the Federal formula is simple and profound. Whether the student has $100 or $10,000 dollars, 20% of the value is assessed and added to the student's contribution. For example, $5,000 has been saved in the student's name and that amount is entered on the FAFSA under student assets. The Expected Family Contribution will increase by $1,000 ($5,000 x 20%). The assessment rate for student assets in the institutional methodology (IM) (school's using the CSS Profile) is 25%. Financial planners, investment advisers, insurance agents and tax preparers generally advise their clients to save money in their children's name to take advantage of lower marginal tax brackets. The average impact of this is about 10% less taxes paid on interest or dividends earned. If the student is eligible for aid, the assessment is 20% of the whole investment plus a possible income assessment from the interest and dividends produced by the investment. The bottom line is, if there is a remote chance of receiving financial aid, do not save money in the student's name.

So where should you save? As you will see shortly, parental assets are assessed at significantly lower rates than student assets, thus college savings plans are much more advantageous when owned by a parent. Colleges requiring the Profile application treat assets of the student's siblings the same way as parental assets, unless the sibling is also in college. Although sibling assets are not included on a federal financial aid form, a younger sibling with assets eventually will encounter financial aid problems when he or she is ready to go to college. Thus, you are better off saving in the parent's name, since the maximum assessment is 5.64% (rather than 20%). This is a serious inequity within the Federal formula. Mr. Green saves $10,000 in his daughter's name and incurs a $2,000 increase to their EFC. Mr. Gray saves $10,000 in his own name and has $564 of assets added to their EFC. Both families made the same sacrifices to help fund their child's education, but because Mr. Green was uninformed, it potentially will cost him $1,436 more than Mr. Gray!

Many clients already have savings programs established for their children and ask what to do with them. If the savings can be legally moved, then move them. I often recommend that students with minimal savings use that money on college supplies that will have to be purchased anyway, rather than list them on a financial aid form. If the student is going to need a car or computer for school, it may be beneficial to make these purchases prior to completing the FAFSA or PROFILE rather than after completion. This strategy may in essence be giving you up to a 20% discount. Assets are valued on financial aid forms at time of application. This is the date you sign and submit the FAFSA. If there is a large sum of money in the student's name that cannot be legally moved (i.e., trusts), then spend it first towards college costs. If you don't, the remaining balance will be reassessed at 20% when you complete the FAFSA for the following year. This brings to mind a case where a financial planner recommended a college savings program for a 10 year old utilizing zero coupon bonds maturing at the beginning of each year of college. The value of each bond at maturity was $4,000. Although the intentions of the planner were admirable, he was not aware of the financial aid implications of his recommendations. The following demonstrates the impact of this plan:

Value of Bonds		Assessment			Aid Reductions
Year 1:	$4,000	X	20%	=	$800
	3,600	X	20%	=	720
	3,200	X	20%	=	640
	2,800	X	20%	=	560
					2,720
Year 2:	4,000	X	20%	=	800
	3,600	X	20%	=	720
	3,200	X	20%	=	640
					2,160
Year 3:	4,000	X	20%	=	800
	3,600	X	20%	=	720
					1,520
Year 4:	4,000	X	20%	=	800

Total Aid Reductions:
      $7,200

Summary: $16,000 Matured bond value
                  - 7,200 Financial aid reductions
             $ 8,800 Net

What the Planner should have done was to invest the bonds in the parent's name or a 529 plan. The financial aid reductions over four years would not have been greater than $2,030.

PARENTAL ASSETS

As previously stated, the maximum Federal assessment on parental assets is approximately 6 percent (5.64 percent to be exact). Let's define what assets are listed on the financial aid form. You must include all cash savings (cash, checking account balances, passbook savings, certificates of deposit, money market accounts, etc.). You must also include the value of your stocks, bonds, mutual funds, and other securities, real estate you own, as well as the net value of a business or farm that you have ownership in. You do not have to include the value of a small business that the student or parents own and controls that has 100 or fewer full-time employees. You do not list consumer assets such as automobiles, furnishings, recreational vehicles, etc. on the FAFSA. You do not include any money held in retirement accounts , life insurance or annuities. The equity in your primary home, as well as a family farm that the family lives on and operates is not an assessable asset for Federal financial aid and should not be listed on the FAFSA. However, many colleges and universities that offer institutional aid are not excluding your home or farm equity from assessments when determining institutional aid eligibility.

Unlike student assets, the "Formula" does not assess parental assets from the first dollar. An Educational Savings and Asset Protection Allowance protects some of your net worth from being considered available for college expenses (See pages 18 and 19). This allowance is based on the age of the oldest parent. As the age of the parent increases, the allowance increases. This may be one of the few times in your life when being older is a benefit. For example, if there are two parents in the household, and the oldest parent is 45 years old, the Asset Protection Allowance is $42,900. If the total value of your assets is $60,000, only $17,100 ($60,000 - $42,900) would be assessed. If there is only one parent in the household and that parent is age 45, the allowance is $14,900. The Asset Protection Allowance for two parents range from $2,500 at age 26, to $74,000 (if the age of the oldest parent is 65 or older).

If you understand this concept, you now know that you need not spend or shelter every dollar of parental savings to maximize aid eligibility, as many people believe they should.

As previously stated, assets that are excluded for Federal purposes include pensions, IRA's, 403B's Keoghs, 401K's, annuities, and the cash value of life insurance policies. Elective pretax contributions to these plans for the tax year being used on the FAFSA will be included as untaxed income, but the value of these assets remains sheltered.

ASSET PROTECTION ALLOWANCE

(TWO PARENTS - DEPENDENT STUDENT)

TOTAL NET VALUE OF ASSETS	$ 50,000
ASSET PROTECTION ALLOWANCE (OLDEST PARENT AGE 45)	- 42,900
AMOUNT OF PARENTAL ASSETS ASSESSED FOR FAMILY CONTRIBUTION	$ 7,100

EDUCATION SAVINGS
AND ASSET PROTECTION ALLOWANCE
DEPENDENT STUDENTS

IF THE AGE OF THE OLDEST PARENT IS:	AND THERE ARE- TWO PARENTS	ONE PARENT
25 or less	$ 0	$ 0
26	2,500	900
27	5,100	1,800
28	7,600	2,700
29	10,200	3,500
30	12,700	4,400
31	15,300	5,300
32	17,800	6,200
33	20,400	7,100
34	22,900	8,000
35	25,500	8,900
36	28,000	9,800
37	30,600	10,600
38	33,100	11,500
39	35,700	12,400
40	38,200	13,300
41	38,900	13,600
42	39,900	13,900
43	40,900	14,200
44	41,900	14,500
45	42,900	14,900
46	44,000	15,200
47	45,100	15,500
48	46,200	15,900
49	47,400	16,300
50	48,800	16,700
51	50,000	17,100
52	51,200	17,500
53	52,800	18,000
54	54,300	18,400
55	55,600	18,800
56	57,300	19,300
57	58,700	19,800
58	60,400	20,300
59	62,200	20,800
60	64,000	21,400
61	65,800	22,000
62	67,700	22,600
63	70,000	23,200
64	72,000	23,800
65 or more	74,000	24,500

ASSET PROTECTION ALLOWANCE
INDEPENDENT STUDENTS

AGE OF STUDENT	ALLOWANCE FOR-	
	MARRIED STUDENT	UNMARRIED STUDENT
25 or less	$ 0	$ 0
26	2,500	900
27	5,100	1,800
28	7,600	2,700
29	10,200	3,500
30	12,700	4,400
31	15,300	5,300
32	17,800	6,200
33	20,400	7,100
34	22,900	8,000
35	25,500	8,900
36	28,000	9,800
37	30,600	10,600
38	33,100	11,500
39	35,700	12,400
40	38,200	13,300
41	38,900	13,600
42	39,900	13,900
43	40,900	14,200
44	41,900	14,500
45	42,900	14,900
46	44,000	15,200
47	45,100	15,500
48	46,200	15,900
49	47,400	16,300
50	48,800	16,700
51	50,000	17,100
52	51,200	17,500
53	52,800	18,000
54	54,300	18,400
55	55,600	18,800
56	57,300	19,300
57	58,700	19,800
58	60,400	20,300
59	62,200	20,800
60	64,000	21,400
61	65,800	22,000
62	67,700	22,600
63	70,000	23,200
64	72,000	23,800
65 or more	74,000	24,500

"Assets?...What Assets?"

SHELTERING ASSETS

Often parents want to shelter some of their savings for other purposes, such as retirement. My first recommendation is investing in fixed annuities. These tax-deferred investments are not assessable for Federal aid and can often be purchased without sales or administrative charges. Annuities follow the 59-1/2 rules. Monies taken out prior to age 59-1/2 are subject to a 10% excise tax, as well as being taxed as ordinary income. An early withdrawal after the student has completed school isn't necessarily disastrous. If after-tax money was invested (which is usually the case), the penalty and taxes is only on the interest earned. If you were eligible for aid and did not shelter assessable assets, you may have lost up to 5.64 percent a year on the your investment. What could be disastrous is if you withdraw money from a pension or annuity when your student is still in college. The entire distribution (taxable and non-taxable) can be considered income for financial aid purposes. Life insurance is another option for sheltering assets, but purchase life insurance only if you have an insurance need. Insurance policies have considerable charges built into their contracts. These expenses will negatively impact your rate of return.

Assets listed on the CSS Profile will include non-qualified annuities and therefore will have no sheltering benefit for colleges requiring that application.

Before investing into any financial aid shelter, seek professional advice regarding any fees, liquidity, tax implications and financial aid implications of early withdrawal.

VALUATION OF ASSETS

Since assets may impact aid eligibility, it is important that they are valued correctly. For most families, the most valuable asset is their home. The CSS Profile and some institutional forms will require you to state how much your home is worth. Do not use assessed or tax value. Your home is worth what someone will pay for it in a reasonable period of time. The appreciation of real property has varied throughout regions on the United States. A good measure of fair market value is comparable home sales in your area. Use a conservative, but realistic home value. Remember your primary residence is excluded on the FAFSA.

Families often erroneously state the amount of savings bonds at their face value. Remember, it takes years for these bonds to mature and your bonds may be currently worth only a fraction of their face value. If you are unsure, you can look them up online at [www.treasurydirect.gov/indiv/tools/tools_savingsbondcalc.htm]. If you own stocks or funds, check their current price the day you complete your form.

Placing a value on a business or rental property should be determined by estimating the fair market value. The business value includes the value of land, buildings, machinery, equipment, inventories, etc., on the day the financial aid form is completed. How much do you think someone would pay you for your business or business property? This number may be contrary to book value or a value established by your accountant. Be sure to offset equity with any debt against the business. It is the net value (fair market value minus debt) that is assessed.

Trust Funds

Trust funds in the name of a specific individual should be reported as that person's assets on the application. In the case of divorce or separation where the trust is owned jointly, and ownership is not being contested, the property and the debt is equally divided between the owners for reporting purposes, unless the terms of the trust specify some other method of division.

As a general rule, the value of the trust must be reported as an asset, even if the beneficiary's access to the trust is restricted. If the grantor of a trust has voluntarily placed restrictions on the use of the trust, then the trust would be reported in the same manner as a trust that did not have any specific restrictions. The way in which the trust must be reported varies according to whether the student (or dependent student's parent) receives or will receive the interest income, the trust principal, or both.

Interest only. If a student, spouse, or parent receives only the interest from the trust, any interest received in the base year must be reported as income. Even if the interest accumulates in the trust and is not paid out during the year, the person who will receive the interest must report an asset value for the interest he or she will receive in the future. The present value of the interest the person will receive while the trust exists can usually be calculated by the trust officer. This value represents the amount a third person would be willing to pay in order to receive the interest income that the student (or parent) will receive from the trust in the future.

Principal only. The student, spouse, or parents who will receive only the trust principal must report the present value of his or her right to the trust principal as an asset. For example, if the principal is $10,000 and reverts to a dependent student's parents when the trust ends in 10 years, but the student is receiving the interest earned from the trust, the present value of the parents' right to the principal of the trust must be reported as a parental asset. The present value of the principal is the amount that a third person would pay at the present time for the right to receive the principal 10 years from now (basically, the amount that one would have to deposit now to receive $10,000 in 10 years, including the accumulated interest). Again, the present value can be calculated by the trust officer.

Both Principal and Interest. If a student, spouse, or parent receives both the interest and principal from the trust, the present value of both interest and principal would be reported, as described above. If the trust is set up in such a manner that the interest accumulates within the trust until the trust ends, the beneficiary should report as an asset the present value of the funds (both interest and principal) that he or she is expected to receive when the trust ends.

If a trust has been restricted by court order, it would not be reported as an asset. One example of such a restricted trust is one that was set up by court order to pay for future surgery for the victim of a car accident.

DEBT

The Formula does take debt into consideration when assessing your assets. Mortgages, home equity loans, and investment debt will offset your assets. Assets minus liabilities equal net worth. If your home is valued at $100,000 and you have a $60,000 mortgage, your net equity is $40,000. The treatment of the equity in your home is no different from money in the bank. As previously mentioned, home equity is not assessed for Federal aid purposes, but is often assessed by schools in determining their own institutional aid eligibility. Consumer debt however, is not considered a liability for financial aid purposes. It often makes a lot of sense to consolidate auto loans, credit card balances, etc. into a home equity loan prior to filing for financial aid. Not only do you increase the potential for more aid eligibility, but you will be paying interest that in most cases is tax deductible and at a lower rate.

MORTGAGES

AND

HOME EQUITY LOANS

<u>REDUCE</u>

PARENTAL NET ASSETS
FOR INSTITUTIONAL AID

AVOID
CONSUMER DEBT!

STUDENT INCOME

Within the Federal formula, both parental and student income is assessed on earnings received during the calendar year preceding the school year that aid is being applied for. This is called "Base-Year Income." As of the date of this publication, $5,250 of student income is protected in the Formula. This number is adjusted annually. Student income above $5,250 is assessed at 50% (after allowances for taxes) and added to the EFC. For example, in January of Molly's senior year in high school, she begins working a part-time job and earns $4,000 by the end of the summer. When she completes her FAFSA for her sophomore year in college, there is no student income assessment since she earned less than $5,250. Student income not only includes earned income, but it may also include investment income (interest, dividends and capital gains). Recall the example of the student who had saved $10,000 in his name and was assessed 20% of the asset. If that student earned 5% on that $10,000 or $500.00, up to 50% of the interest income could have been added to the student contribution if the student's total income exceeded the $5,250. Many colleges that offer institutional aid and use the CSS Profile application, will include a student contribution from income ($1,800 – $2,400) to their own institutional EFC, regardless of whether the student worked or not. Since the majority of student's earn less than the protected amount, in most cases there is no reason for a student not to work, providing they have the time and opportunity. It is important to note that earnings from Federal Work-Study programs are excluded from student income assessments. These earnings are taxable, but will not negatively impact future financial aid eligibility.

PARENTAL INCOME

The best piece of advice I can give regarding parental income is: Don't quit your day job! After allowances against income, the assessment on parental income can range from zero to 47%. The rate is based on the principle that as income increases beyond the amount needed to maintain a basic standard of living, the portion used for family maintenance decreases, while the portion available for discretionary purposes increases. Since the highest offset is less than 50%, you will be better off with an aid reduction than not earning that extra dollar. It is important to note that adjusted gross income is a key factor in the formula. Business or rental losses that flow to page one of your IRS Form 1040 are helpful. Large capital gains and/or withdrawing money from IRA's and pension plans will increase your taxable income and decrease your need. If you can avoid either of them, you may save yourself a ton of money. I recently completed financial aid forms for a family that withdrew $20,000 from an IRA to pay tuition. Although there was no early distribution penalty since the money was used for college tuition, the end result was nearly $7,000 in tax liabilities and a $6,000 reduction in financial aid. That was not a cost-effective decision.

As with student income, unearned income (interest, dividends, capital gains, etc.) is treated the same as earned income. The money growing tax-deferred in your IRA or 401K, etc., is not counted, but you must include your elective contributions to these plans as untaxed income on the financial aid forms. You do not include employer contributions to your retirement. Tax-free income derived from municipal bonds are also assessed and must be included on the FAFSA. Remember, the tax-deferred asset is not included on the form, but the pre-tax contribution to that asset is treated as untaxed income.

For example, each year Mr. Smith contributes $2,600 (pretax) to his 401K plan at work. The current value of his retirement plan is $30,000. Mr. Smith must list $2,600 as untaxed income on the FAFSA, but does not have to include his $30,000 balance as an asset

How Parental Income Is Factored

TAXABLE INCOME:
- Wages, Salaries, Tips
- Interest Income
- Dividend Income
- Net Income (or Loss) from a business, farm, rents, etc
- Other Taxable Income (alimony, capital gains, pensions, etc.)

+

NON-TAXABLE INCOME:
- Deductible IRA and/or Keogh Payments
- Untaxed Portions of Pensions
- Tax-Exempt Interest Income
- Payments to Tax-Deferred Pension and Savings Plans
- Worker's Compensation
- Disability Benefits
- Child Support

= TOTAL INCOME

ALLOWANCES AGAINST PARENT'S INCOME:
- U.S. Income Taxes Paid
- State and Local Tax Allowance
- Social Security Taxes
- Income Protection Allowance (based on family size)
- Employment Expense Allowance
- Education Credits
- Child Support Paid

= TOTAL ALLOWANCES

TOTAL INCOME

- TOTAL ALLOWANCES

AVAILABLE INCOME

"Hail Alma Mater..."

NUMBER OF FAMILY MEMBERS ATTENDING SCHOOL

As previously stated, the Expected Family Contribution is comprised of the parent contribution and the student contribution. You report on the FAFSA how many family members will be attending college at least half time (excluding parents). The more family members attending, the lower the EFC. For example: Christopher is going to college next year and his twin sister Traci is contemplating postponing college for a year. The cost of the college Chris will attend is $19,000. The expected family contribution for Chris is $20,000, $19,200 from the parents and $800 from the student. With the exception of a student loan there will be no need-based aid eligibility for Chris. If Christopher's sister decides not to postpone attending college for a year, the parent contribution would halve ($19,200 divided by 2). The parent contribution would be $9,600 plus $800 from Chris for an EFC of $10,400. Now Chris is eligible for $8,600 of aid. Traci's contribution from her parents would be $9,600 plus any contribution from her income or assets. A family member is considered a student if they will attend an accredited school half-time for at least one term, working towards a degree or certificate leading to a recognized education credential.

Although Traci's enrollment will certainly increase Christopher's Federal aid eligibility, there is no warranty that the school is going to increase his aid with their own institutional funds. Although many schools financially recognize more than one sibling in school when formulating financial aid packages, it is ultimately up to the individual college to determine how much more aid they will offer when another sibling is going to college.

Remember - a parent attending college does not impact the student's federal financial aid.

CHAPTER
THREE

SPECIAL
CONSIDERATIONS

DEADLINES

Colleges and universities require that financial aid forms be completed and received at the appropriate processing center by a specific date. This date (for Federal aid) will be after January 1st of the same year preceding the fall semester. It is important to adhere to these deadlines to ensure that you don't lose the opportunity to receive any aid you could be eligible for. If the student is applying to schools with different aid deadlines, be certain to file the forms prior to the earliest deadline. These filing deadlines also apply to the College Board Profile application, required by certain schools in addition to the FAFSA. If a student is applying "early decision", it is important to contact the school and verify what form(s) they require and when they should be submitted. Early decision deadlines are usually in the fall of the student's senior year in high school. Applying early decision may give you an admissions edge, but I have seen little (if any) financial aid benefit to early decision applicants.

A problem many families are faced with is the inability to complete their income tax forms by the aid deadline. Some schools require that the financial aid forms be submitted as early as January 15th. W-2 and 1099 forms usually haven't been received by this date, so it is impossible to complete your taxes. If you are faced with early deadlines, you will need to estimate your tax return and use the estimated figures on your financial aid forms. You will then check the box on the form stating that you will file a tax return, but haven't yet. If possible, use information from a completed tax return;

however, do not miss deadlines because your taxes are not completed. When estimating taxes, use your last pay stub to determine income, check bankbooks to see how much interest was earned and approximate your itemized deductions. Since tax tables change every year, use current tables to determine your taxes paid. A common mistake in completing the line, "Taxes Paid" is entering how much tax was withheld from your earnings. "Taxes Paid" is your tax liability based on your taxable income. This number is derived from the tax schedules.

A final note concerning deadlines: The sooner you can complete and mail your financial aid forms prior to the deadline, the better. The early bird may get the fattest worm.

DEPENDENT VERSUS INDEPENDENT

When a student is classified as independent, parental income and assets are not assessed in the Federal formula. Obviously, if parents have high income and assets, there is a strong advantage not to include parental information on a financial aid form. The misinformation for determining independence for financial aid is is sometimes incredulous. The most commonly asked question is, "If I don't claim my son or daughter on my tax return, or if I throw them out of the house, they will be emancipated, right?" Wrong! If it were that simple, we would all throw our kids out.

For Federal financial aid purposes, the student must meet specific criteria to be considered independent. Yes to any one of the following questions will qualify a student as an independent:

- ➤ Were you born before January 1, 1988? (This is for 2011-12. For the 2012-2013 academic year it will be January 1, 1989 etc.).
- ➤ As of today, are you married? (Also answer "Yes" if you are separated but not divorced.)
- ➤ At the beginning of the 2010–2011 school year, will you be working on a master's or doctorate program (such as an MA, MBA, MD, JD, PhD, EdD, graduate certificate, etc.)?

- Are you currently serving on active duty in the U.S. Armed Forces for purposes other than training?

- Are you a veteran of the U.S. Armed Forces?

- Do you have children who will receive more than half of their support from you now and the next academic year?

- Do you have dependents (other than your children or spouse) who live with you and who receive more than half of their support from you now and the next academic year?

- At any time since you turned age 13, were both your parents deceased, were you in foster care or were you a dependent or ward of the court?.

- Are you or were you an emancipated minor as determined by a court in your state of legal residence?

- Are you or were you in legal guardianship as determined by a court in your state of legal residence?

- At any time on or after July 1, 2010, did your high school or school district homeless liaison determine that you were an unaccompanied youth who was homeless?

- At any time on or after July 1, 2010, did the director of an emergency shelter or transitional housing program funded by the U.S. Department of Housing and Urban Development determine that you were an unaccompanied youth who was homeless?

- At any time on or after July 1, 2010, did the director of a runaway or homeless youth basic center or transitional living program determine that you were an unaccompanied youth who was homeless or were self-supporting and at risk of being homeless?

It should be noted that the criteria for establishing independence for Federal aid might be different than the criteria for establishing independence for state or institutional aid. Check with your State and college and ask what guidelines they have for independent status.

The financial aid administrator may override the student's dependency status in individual cases if he or she decides that the student should be considered independent. This generally occurs in only extreme cases and should not be anticipated.

"Does this mean I'm independent?"

SINGLE PARENTS - REMARRIED PARENTS

One of the more confusing aspects for parents when completing the financial aid form occurs when the student's parents are separated or divorced. Dealing with this issue for Federal aid purposes is actually quite simple. List only the financial information from the custodial parent on the Federal financial aid form. The custodial parent is the parent with whom the student lived with the most during the last twelve months. If the custodial parent is remarried, the income and assets of the spouse are included. The next section will provide more detail defining who is a parent. Certain colleges may also require a Divorced/Separated Parent's Statement to be completed by the non-custodial parent. The colleges that require non-custodial parent information are generally colleges that use the CSS Profile application. This information may impact institutional aid eligibility, but does not necessarily mean the school will add the income and assets of both households together to determine financial aid eligibility. The school's rationale is both parents should be responsible for a contribution towards their child's education.

WHO IS CONSIDERED A PARENT?

The term "parent" is not restricted to biological parents. There are instances (such as when a grandparent legally adopts the applicant) in which a person other than a biological parent is treated as a parent, and in these instances, the parental questions on the application must be answered, since they apply to such an individual (or individuals).

If your parents are both living and married to each other, answer the questions about both of them.

If your parents are living together and have not been formally married but meet the criteria in their state for a common-law-marriage, they should report their status as married on the application. If the state does not consider their situation to be a common-law-marriage, then you should follow the rules for

---

divorced parents. Check with the appropriate state agency concerning the definition of a common-law-marriage.

A foster parent, legal guardian, or a grandparent or other relative is not treated as a parent for a purposes of filing a FAFSA unless that person has legally adopted the applicant. An adoptive parent is treated in the same manner as a biological parent on the FAFSA.

If one, but not both, of your parents has died, you should answer the parental questions about the surviving parent. Do not report any financial information for the deceased parent on the FAFSA. If the surviving parent dies after the FAFSA has been filed, you must submit a correction, thus updating your dependency status to independent, and correct all other information as appropriate. If the surviving parent is remarried as of the date you complete the FAFSA, answer the questions about both the parent and the person he or she married (your stepparent).

If your parents are divorced or separated, answer the questions about the parent you lived with more during the 12 months preceding the date you complete the FAFSA. If you do not live with one parent more than the other, give answers about the parents who provided more financial support during the 12 months preceding the date you complete the FAFSA, or during the most recent year that you actually received support from a parent. If your parents are legally separated, the same rules apply for a divorced couple are used to determine which parents information must be reported. A couple doesn't have to be legally separated in order to be considered separated for purposes of the FAFSA. The couple may consider themselves informally separated when one of the partners has left the household for an indefinite period of time. If the partners live together, they can't be considered informally separated even if they still live together.

A stepparent is treated in the same manner as a biological parent if the stepparent is married, as of the date of application , to the biological parent whose information will be reported on the FAFSA, or if the stepparent has legally adopted you. There are no exceptions. Prenuptial agreements do not exempt the stepparent from providing required data on the FAFSA. Note that the stepparent's income information for the entire base year must be reported even if your parent and stepparent were not married until after the start of year, but were married prior to the date the FAFSA was completed.

Parent's marital status is as of the day you complete the FAFSA. The FAFSA asks about parents' marital status because their marital status directly affects the treatment of income and assets in the EFC calculation.

In the event that a separation, divorce or death occurred in the year prior to applying for financial aid, and a joint income tax return is filed, only the income of the custodial or surviving parent is entered on the financial aid forms. The custodial parent should only list his or her portion of assets and liabilities. For example, if the parent's vacation home is valued at $100,000 with a mortgage balance of $60,000 (assuming 50% ownership), the custodial parent would list his or her portion of the equity in the home, in this case $20,000.

SPECIAL SITUATIONS

If there is something significant that will impact your ability to pay towards your student's education that is not reflected on the FAFSA, you should communicate that information with the financial aid officer at the college your student will be or is attending. Issues such as high medical and dental expenses, elementary or secondary private school tuition (for children other than the applicant), loss of employment, or been notified that you will be laid off, or have any other extraordinary financial or personal circumstances (death or divorce) that will impact your ability to pay college costs, contact the financial aid administrator at the school the student is or will be attending. The financial aid officer can use "professional judgment" on a case-by-case basis to adjust data items in the Formula.

Case One: A family with $6,000 of non-reimbursed medical expenses has an adjusted gross income of $30,000. The aid administrator might decide to adjust the reported AGI to take into account these unusually high expenses.

Case Two: A parent has been notified that he will be laid off in the imminent future. The aid administrator may decide to substitute expected income for the upcoming year rather than use the previous years income. In this case, be prepared (prior to contacting the school) to estimate how much income (including unemployment benefits) the family expects to receive as well as how much federal tax you anticipate paying for that year.

Since professional judgment involves a certain degree of subjectivity, students applying to a number of schools should make all aid administrators aware of their circumstances. You will find that some schools will be more flexible and generous than others.

"Maybe I should go to college to learn how to do these forms."

THE PROCESS

COMPLETING THE FINANCIAL AID FORMS

To be considered for virtually any type of financial aid, a financial aid form must be filled out and sent to a centralized processing center. Most people find the financial aid forms confusing; so don't feel too inadequate if you are experiencing difficulty completing them. It is extremely important to complete these forms correctly and have them processed on time. Financial aid forms that are rejected and sent back to the applicant may ultimately miss deadlines and thus jeopardize aid.

If there are professionals in your area that specialize in form completion, it may be well worth your while to employ them. Some college financial aid offices may offer help with the forms (particularly if the student is applying to that school). Your tax preparer will understand the income elements that need to be completed, but don't expect him or her to have a vast background in the intricacies of financial aid. Remember, aid eligibility will be determined by the information submitted on the financial aid forms.

All students applying for Federal financial aid must complete the Free Application For Federal Student Aid (FAFSA). This form, in most cases, is filed online using FAFSA On The Web [www.fafsa.ed.gov]. In addition to the FAFSA, cetain schools will also require the completion of the College Scholarship Service (CSS) Profile application. CSS is part of the College Board. To determine whether the Profile form is necessary, see if the school is listed on the College Board website [https://profileonline.collegeboard.com/prf/index.jsp] . If the school is listed, the Profile is required. If the school is not listed, only the FAFSA is required. If the student is applying to multiple schools and only some schools require the Profile, the student should list only those schools with code numbers on the Profile form, but list all schools on the FAFSA. The reason many colleges require the Profile in addition to the FAFSA is to further qualify the student for institutional aid eligibility. One of the more significant items that is asked for on the Profile and not on the FAFSA is home value and debt. The Profile schools generally treat the equity in your home as an asset, thus creating the potential for less aid eligibility.

The following section contains some important points to remember when completing the FAFSA.

Getting Your Federal Student Aid PIN

What is a Federal Student Aid PIN and what is it used for?

Your PIN is an electronic access code that serves as your personal identifier. Your PIN allows you to:

- "Sign" your FAFSA electronically and complete the student aid process completely online—no paper is involved. If you're a dependent student and one of your parents has a Federal Student Aid PIN, he or she can sign your FAFSA electronically online as well.

- Correct your FAFSA online.

- Access your *Student Aid Report** (SAR).

- "Sign" a master promissory note* for a federal student loan.

- Access your federal student aid records online, including your student loan history information on NSLDS.*

To apply for your PIN, go to [www.pin.ed.gov].

In addition to applying for you PIN on this web site, you can also *Check your Pin Status, Request a Duplicate PIN, Access your Pin E-mail, Change your PIN, Update your Personal Information, Disable your PIN, Reestablish your PIN and Activate your PIN.*

If you are a dependent student, one parent should also apply for a PIN to electronically sign the FAFSA, as well as to electronically sign a Master Promissory Note should they elect to apply for a PLUS Loan.

HOW DO I APPLY FOR FEDERAL STUDENT AID?

Step 1 ➢ Get a PIN, a personal identification number. A PIN lets you apply, "sign" your online FAFSA, make corrections to your application information, and more-all online.

Step 2 ➢ Collect the documents needed to apply, including income tax returns and W-2 forms (and other records of income). A full list of what you need is at www.fafsa.ed.gov. If your tax return is not complete at the time you apply, estimate the tax information, apply, and correct the information later.

Step 3 ➢ Complete the Free Application for Federal Student Aid as soon as possible after Jan. 1 to meet school and state aid deadlines. Apply online at www.fafsa.ed.gov,

Step 4 ➢ Review your Student Aid Report (SAR)-the result of your FAFSA application. If necessary, make changes or corrections online and resubmit your SAR for reprocessing. Your complete, correct SAR will contain your Expected Family Contribution (EFC)-the number used to determine your federal student aid eligibility.

Step 5 ➢ If you are selected for verification, your school's financial aid office will ask you to submit tax returns and other documents, as appropriate. Be sure to meet the school's deadline, or the aid package will be postponed or reduced.

Step 6   ➢Whether you're selected for verification or not, make sure the financial aid office at the school has all the information needed to determine your eligibility.

Step 7   ➢All students: Contact the financial aid office if you have any questions about the aid being offered.

First-time applicants: Review award letters from schools to compare amounts and types of aid being offered. Decide which school to attend based on a combination of (a) how well the school suits your needs and (b) its affordability after all aid is taken into account.

FAFSA INSTRUCTIONS

Are You Eligible for Federal Student Aid?

In general, to receive aid from the federal student aid programs, you must meet the following requirements:

Be a U.S. citizen or eligible noncitizen.

Have a high school diploma, General Educational Development (GED) certificate, pass an approved "ability to benefit" test, or have completed a high school education in a home school setting that is recognized as a home school or private school under state law.

Enroll in an eligible program as a regular student seeking a degree or certificate.

Be registered with Selective Service if required (in general, if you are a male age 18 through 25).

Meet satisfactory academic progress standards set by your school.

Certify that you are not in default on a federal loan or owe money on a federal grant.

Certify that you will use federal student aid only for educational purposes.

And, only if you have previously received federal student aid:

Certify that you were not convicted for a drug offense that occurred while you were enrolled in school and receiving federal student aid.

First Section of the FAFSA

Purpose: These questions collect personal identification information (name, telephone number, address, Social Security number and so on). Also included is a question about citizenship status because you must be a U.S. citizen or eligible noncitizen to receive federal student aid.

Name. The Department matches each name and Social Security number (SSN) with the Social Security Administration (SSA). Therefore, the name provided here should match the name on your Social Security card.

Permanent mailing address. You must give a permanent home mailing address (not a school or office address).

Social Security number. Generally, you must have an SSN to be eligible for federal student financial aid. If you submit a FAFSA without an SSN, your FAFSA will be returned to you unprocessed.

Your date of birth. Enter in the appropriate boxes of the paper FAFSA the month, day, and year in which you were born (formatted as MMDDYYYY).

Your permanent telephone number. Enter your permanent telephone number where you can be contacted.

Driver's license number and state. You should provide your driver's license number (if any). If you do not have a driver's license, leave Questions 11 and 12 blank.

E-mail address. If you enter your e-mail address here the processor will send you information electronically, such as notification that your FAFSA was received.

Citizenship status. You can receive federal student financial aid only if you are a U.S. citizen or an eligible noncitizen. If you have changed from a noncitizen to a citizen and have not informed the SSA, contact the SSA to update your status. Otherwise, the SSA may report that you are not a citizen, and you will have to provide citizenship documentation before receiving aid.

For financial aid purposes, an eligible noncitizen is one of the following:

A U.S. permanent resident who has a Permanent Resident Card (I-551 or I-151)

A conditional permanent resident (I-551C)

A noncitizen with an Arrival-Departure Record (I-94) from the Department of Homeland Security (DHS) (specifically, the U.S. Citizenship and Immigration Services) showing any one of the following designations: "Refugee," "Asylum Granted," "Parole" (the I-94 must confirm 'paroled for a minimum of 1-year status' has not expired), or "Cuban-Haitian Entrant"

If you are neither a citizen nor an eligible noncitizen, you are not eligible for federal student aid.

Alien Registration Number (A-Number). If you are an eligible noncitizen, enter your eight- or nine-digit A-Number. Leave the first space blank if you have an eight-digit A-Number.

Marital status. Your marital status directly affects how your income and assets are treated in the EFC calculation. You must report your marital status as of the date the application is submitted. An applicant cannot update FAFSA information for changes in marital status after the application is filed.

Date of marital status. You should enter the date (the month and the year) you married, divorced, separated, or were widowed. If you never married, leave this question blank.

State of legal residence. The Department will disclose your FAFSA information to state agencies in your state of legal residence, to each school listed on the FAFSA, and to state agencies in the state in which each school is located. State and institutional programs may use the information provided on the FAFSA to determine your eligibility for state and institutional aid.

Your state of legal residence is also used in the EFC calculation to determine the appropriate allowance for state and other taxes paid by that state's residents.

Your residence is your true, fixed, and permanent home. If you are a dependent student, the state of legal residence is usually the state in which your parents live. If you moved from your family's state of residence into a state for the sole purpose of attending a college, do not count the state to which you moved as your legal residence.

Are you male? To receive federal student financial aid, male students who are 18 through 25 years old and born after December 31, 1959 must be registered with Selective Service. Indicate whether you are male.

Selective Service registration. If you are male, 18 through 25 years of age, and have not registered with Selective Service, you can enter "Yes" and Selective Service will register you. You can also register on the Web at www.sss.gov

Degree or certificate. Indicate the one-digit code for the expected degree or certificate you will be working on during the upcoming school year, using the "Degree/Certificate Code List" below. If your degree or certificate does not fit any of these categories, or if you are undecided, enter "9.

Grade level during upcoming school year. Enter appropriate year. Grade level does not mean the number of years you have attended college, but grade level in regard to completing your degree/certificate.

High school diploma/GED. If you will receive your high school diploma or earn a General Education Development (GED)

certificate or equivalent home school credential before you enroll in college for the upcoming school year, answer "Yes" to this question. Otherwise, answer "No."

1st bachelor's degree. This question has a direct bearing on your eligibility for Federal Pell Grants and Federal Supplemental Educational Opportunity Grants, which are restricted to students who have not yet received bachelor's degrees. (The only exception is that certain students who already have a bachelor's degree and are now taking courses for teacher certification may receive a Federal Pell Grant.) You must answer "Yes" to this question if you have (or will have by July 1st) a degree from a college in the U.S., or an equivalent degree from a college in another country.

Father's/mother's highest school level. These questions do not affect your eligibility for federal student aid. Some state and institutional programs use the information provided here to offer aid to first-generation college students.

Illegal drug offenses. If you have been convicted of possessing or selling illegal drugs while you were receiving federal student aid (grants, loans, or work-study) answer yes and further questions will be asked to determine if you can receive federal aid.

If you have a conviction, you should still complete and submit the FAFSA because even if you are ineligible for federal student aid, you might still be eligible for state or institutional aid. Many states and schools use the data supplied by the FAFSA to determine students' eligibility for aid from those non-federal entities.

Are you planning to complete coursework necessary to become an elementary or secondary school teacher, either now or in the future? The Teacher Education Assistance for College and Higher Education (TEACH) Grant Program provides grants to students enrolled in a participating college who intend to teach in a public or private elementary or secondary school that serves students from low-income families.

Answer "Yes" to learn more about the TEACH Grant. A "Yes" answer indicates to the schools listed on your FAFSA that you are interested in completing the necessary coursework to become a teacher. Answering "Yes" to this question does not guarantee you will obtain aid from the new federal program.

College Releases
This section permits the student to list up to ten colleges on the FAFSA that he or she may attend. Students can send information to additional schools by adding the new colleges using FAFSA On The Web "add or delete a school code"[fafsa.ed.gov].

How To Complete the Income Tax Section. (Instructions apply to both parent and student income).
The Income entered on a FAFSA is what is called the base year income. This is the tax year that precedes the FAFSA year. For example for a 2012-2013 FAFSA, you would be using 2011 tax information. To avoid missing deadlines you can use estimated income figures when completing the FAFSA.

If you are married at the time you submit the FAFSA, both your and your spouse's income, assets, and exemptions must be reported. If you and your spouse filed (or will file) separate tax returns, be sure to include the combined information from both returns on the FAFSA.

If you are single, divorced, separated, or widowed, you must answer the questions for yourself only and ignore the references on the FAFSA to "spouse."

If you are divorced, separated, or widowed but filed (or will file) a joint tax return, you must give only your portion of the exemptions, income, and taxes paid for the income and asset questions.

Foreign Income
Income earned in a foreign country is treated the same as income earned in the U.S. Convert all figures to U.S. dollars, using the exchange rate in effect on the day you fill out the FAFSA.

Income Section (Student and Parents)

Type of return filed. Indicate which IRS tax form you filed or will file.

Eligible to file a 1040A or 1040EZ. Indicate your eligibility to file one of these forms (even if you filed or will file an IRS Form 1040).

For instance, tax preparers often file a Form 1040 or an electronic 1040 on behalf of a tax filer, even though that person's income and tax filing circumstances would allow him or her to file a 1040A or 1040EZ.

In general, you are eligible to file a 1040A or 1040EZ if you make less than $100,000, do not itemize deductions, do not receive income from your own business or farm, and do not receive alimony. You are not eligible to file a 1040A or a 1040EZ form if you itemize deductions, receive self-employment income or alimony, or are required to file Schedule D for capital gains. If you filed a 1040 only to claim Hope or Lifetime Learning credits and you would have otherwise been eligible to file a 1040A or 1040EZ, you should answer "Yes" to this question.

Adjusted Gross Income. Provide your (and your spouse's) adjusted gross income (AGI). AGI is found on IRS Form 1040, 1040A or 1040EZ. If you have not completed a tax form, you should calculate your AGI using the instructions for the applicable IRS form.

Note that AGI includes more than just wages earned; for example, alimony, taxable portions of Social Security, and business income are also included.

Income tax. Enter your (and your spouse's) income tax from IRS Form 1040.

Do not copy the amount of federal income tax withheld from a W-2 Form. Do not include any FICA, self-employment, or other taxes. If you did not pay any income tax, enter zero (0).

Exemptions. Enter your (and your spouse's) exemptions.

If you are divorced, separated, or widowed, and have filed or will file a joint tax return, you should give only your portion of the exemptions.

Income earned from working. When the Department's processor calculates your EFC, certain allowances are deducted from your (and your spouse's) income for necessary expenses (such as taxes and basic living costs). Your (and your spouse's) income earned from work (wages, salaries, tips, combat pay) will be used in the EFC calculation as an income factor when no tax form is filed.

If you did not file a tax return, you should report your earnings from work. You can find this information on your W-2 Form(s).

Untaxed Income

Untaxed income benefits are added to the student or parent(s) taxable income to determine total income.

Any employee contributions to an IRA, Keogh, 401K, 403B, or 457 which results in a reduction in your taxable income will be included as untaxed income.

Housing allowances provided to the parents or student, tax-exempt interest, child support received for all children, Worker's Compensation and the untaxed portions of pensions are also included as untaxed income. Contributions to, or payments from, flexible spending arrangements (e.g., cafeteria plans) are not included as untaxed income.

Exclusions From Income

Education credits, child support paid and income from Federal Work Study programs are treated as subtractions from income within the need analysis formula. You do not include any of the following as income:

Subsidized Housing. Rent subsidies paid by government and charitable organizations for low-income housing are not reported as untaxed income.

Forced Sale Proceeds. Income received from the sale of farm or business assets should not be reported if the sale results from a voluntary or involuntary foreclosure, forfeiture, bankruptcy, or an involuntary liquidation.

Miscellaneous

Don't include student aid, earned income credit, additional child tax credit, welfare payments, untaxed Social Security benefits, Supplemental Security Income, Workforce Investment Act educational benefits, on-base military housing or a military housing allowance, combat pay, benefits from flexible spending arrangements (for example, cafeteria plans), foreign income exclusion or credit for federal tax on special fuels. Food Stamps, heating/fuel assistance, and childcare benefits are not counted as income.

QUESTIONS REGARDING INDEPENDENCE

If the student can answer yes to any of the questions regarding independence (i.e. was the student born before a certain date), he or she does not have to complete the parent section of the FAFSA. For more information on dependent-independent status, refer to refer to the section of this book.

PARENT INFORMATION

Who is considered a parent?
The term "parent" is not restricted to biological parents. There are instances (such as when a grandparent legally adopts the applicant) in which a person other than a biological parent is treated as a parent, and in these instances, the parental questions on the application must be answered, since they apply to such an individual (or individuals).
If your parents are both living and married to each other, answer the questions about both of them.
If your parents are living together and have not been formally married but meet the criteria in their state for a common-law marriage, they should report their status as married on the application. If the state does not consider their situation to be a common-law marriage, then you should follow the rules for divorced parents. Check with the appropriate state agency concerning the definition of a common-law marriage.

A foster parent, legal guardian or a grandparent or other relative is not treated as a parent for purposes of filing a FAFSA unless that person has legally adopted the applicant. An adoptive parent is treated in the same manner as a biological parent on the FAFSA.

If one, but not both, of your parents has died, you should answer the parental questions about the surviving parent. Do not report any financial information for the deceased parent on the FAFSA. If the surviving parent dies after the FAFSA has been filed, you must submit a correction, thus updating your dependency status to independent, and correct all other information as appropriate (for example, you will no longer fill out the parent section. If the surviving parent is remarried as of the date you complete the FAFSA, answer the questions about both that parent and the person he or she married (your stepparent).

If your parents are divorced (or separated — see below for more information), answer the questions about the parent you lived with more during the 12 months preceding the date you complete the FAFSA. If you did not live with one parent more than the other, give answers about the parent who provided more financial support during the 12 months preceding the date you complete the FAFSA, or during the most recent year that you actually received support from a parent. If this parent has remarried as of the date you fill out the FAFSA, answer the questions on the remaining sections of the FAFSA about that parent and the person he or she married (your stepparent).

If your parents are legally separated, the same rules that apply for a divorced couple are used to determine which parent's information must be reported. A couple doesn't have to be legally separated in order to be considered separated for purposes of the FAFSA. The couple may consider themselves informally separated when one of the partners has permanently left the household. If the partners live together, they can't be considered informally separated.

52

A stepparent is treated in the same manner as a biological parent if the stepparent is married, as of the date of application, to the biological parent whose information will be reported on the FAFSA, or if the stepparent has legally adopted you. There are no exceptions. Prenuptial agreements do not exempt the stepparent from providing required data on the FAFSA. Note that the stepparent's income information for the entire year prior to application, 2009, must be reported even if your parent and stepparent were not married until after the start of 2009, but were married prior to the date the FAFSA was completed.

Parents' marital status as of today. The FAFSA asks about parents' marital status because their marital status directly affects the treatment of income and assets in the EFC calculation. Your parents must report their marital status as of the date the application is completed.

Month and year your parents where married, separated, divorced, or widowed. Enter the month and year that your parents attained the status you selected.

Parent's Social Security number. Enter your father's/ stepfather's and mother's/stepmother's Social Security number (SSN) (that is, enter the information for the same person whose financial information you are reporting). All dependent applicants must provide the Social Security number of the parent(s) providing financial data on the application. The Privacy Act statement on the FAFSA explains how his SSN can be used. If your father or mother doesn't have a Social Security number, enter 000-00-0000. FAFSA on the Web filers should enter the numbers without dashes.

Parent's last name, first initial, and Date of Birth. Enter your father's/ stepfather's and mother's/stepmother's last name, first initial and date of birth (that is, enter the information for the same person whose financial information you are reporting). Use the name found on his Social Security card. The parent's SSN, last name, and first initial on the application must match the number and name on the Social Security card. For information on how to update or correct a name on your Social Security card, you can call the Social Security Administration (SSA) at 1-800-772-1213 or go to the SSA's Web site at www.ssa.gov

Number in parents' household. The number of family members reported determines the amount of an allowance that protects a portion of the reported income and this amount is subtracted from your family's income in the EFC calculation. This allowance provides for basic living expenses for the household size you indicate in this question.

The following persons are included in your parents' household size:

You (the student), even if you do not live with your parents

Your parents (the ones whose information is reported on the FAFSA)

Your parents' other children, if your parents will provide more than half of their support for the upcoming academic year

Your parents' unborn child, if that child will be born before July 1, preceding the upcoming academic year.

Other people (including your children and/or your unborn child due before July 1), if they live with and receive more than half of their support from your parents at the time of application and will continue to receive that support for the next academic year. To determine whether to include children in the household size, the "support" test is used (rather than a residency requirement) because there may be situations in which a parent supports a child who does not live with the parent, especially in cases where the parent is divorced or separated. In such cases, the parent who provides more than half of the child's support may claim the child in his or her household size. It does not matter what parent claims the child as a dependent for tax purposes.

Support includes money, gifts, loans, housing, food, clothes, car payments or expenses, medical and dental care, and payment of college costs.

Number of college students in parents' household. This question asks about the number of household members who are or will be enrolled in a postsecondary school. Count yourself as a college student. Include others only if they will be attending at least half time in an approved program that leads to a degree or certificate at a postsecondary school eligible to participate in any of the federal student aid programs. Do not include your parents. Also do not include a student at a U.S. military academy because the family is not expected to contribute to their academy student's postsecondary education.

The number of family members in college directly affects your family's ability to contribute to your education costs. For a dependent student, the parents' contribution to the EFC is roughly divided by the number of family members (excluding parents) in college.

Income Section (Student and Parents)

An asset is property owned by the family that has an exchange value. Possessions such as a car, media equipment, clothes or furniture are not reported as assets on financial aid forms.

Part Ownership of An Asset. If the parent or student only has part ownership of the asset, only that part should be reported.

Contested Ownership. Assets should not be reported if the ownership is being contested. For instance, if the parents are separated and they may not sell or borrow against jointly-owned property that is being contested, the responsible parent would not list any value for the property or debts against it. However, if the ownership of the property were not being contested, the property would be reported as an asset.

Cash, Savings and Checking. Enter value of these accounts as of the date you sign the FAFSA.

Other Real Estate and Investment Value. "Investments" include a wide range of securities, including trust funds, money market funds, certificates of deposit, stocks, savings bonds, mutual funds, installment and land sale contracts, commodities, and precious and strategic metals. Investments also include money loaned out by the student or parent. Real estate includes second or summer homes or rental properties. The value of your primary residence should not be included on the FAFSA. The value of real estate and investments is the fair market value at the time the application was signed and dated. Any debt associated with assessable assets is subtracted from the value to determine net equity. Do not include the cash value of life insurance, annuities, IRA's, pensions, etc.

Business. Do not include the value of a small business that the student or parent owns and controls and that has fewer than 100 employees. Otherwise, report the current market value of a business, including land, buildings, machinery, equipment, inventories, etc. Don't include the home, even if it is part of the business. Then subtract what is owed on the business, including the unpaid mortgage and related debts.

Farm. When reporting the current market value of a farm, include the value of the land, buildings, machinery, equipment, livestock, and inventories. The amount of farm debt subtracted should include the unpaid mortgage and related debts, as well as any loan for which the farm assets were used as collateral. Do not include a family farm if it is your principal place of residence and you claimed on Schedule F of the tax return that you "materially participated in the farm's operation."

Preparer's Use Only. If someone other than you, your spouse, or parents completed this form on your behalf, the law requires the preparer to complete and sign this section.

Submitting the Form. Double-check your FAFSA to make sure it is complete and accurate. FAFSA On The Web may be signed via a PIN, a printed signature page or electing to sign the SAR after the FAFSA has been processed.

Although parental information must be provided for a dependent student, a third party (such as another relative, a counselor, or a financial aid administrator) may sign the application in place of the parent if the parent is not currently in the United States, the current address of the parent is not known; or the parent has been determined physically or mentally incapable of providing a signature.

THE FINANCIAL AID PROFILE APPLICATION

In addition to the FAFSA, many private colleges and universities require the College Scholarship Service (CSS) Profile application to be completed. The objective of this form is to help eliminate the need for individual institutional aid forms and to provide a questionnaire that will meet the needs of all schools offering institutional aid. In addition to the basic application, each participating school may choose from a large bank of supplemental questions designed to qualify the student for that school's grants and scholarships. To determine what colleges require this form, a student can obtain a Profile Registration Guide from their high school guidance office or view the participation schools and programs on line at https://profileonline.collegeboard.com/index.jsp.

A student must register on-line to complete the Profile. To register for and complete the CSS/PROFILE online, you first must sign in at collegeboard.com. If the student has already created an account for the SAT, he or she can use the same username and password to log on, otherwise the student must first register with CSS. After the student is logged on, he or she should register to complete the Profile. The registration consists of a handful of questions and then directs the student to select what school(s) is to receive the information. Upon completion of the registration, the student or preparer may complete the application. CSS charges a fee to process this form based on the number of schools selected. If the school the student is applying to does not appear in the Profile registration packet, it is assumed that school does not require this form The CSS Profile may be completed as early as the fall of the student's senior year in high school, whereas the FAFSA cannot be submitted until after January 1st.

THE INSTITUTIONAL FINANCIAL AID FORM

In addition to the FAFSA, and sometimes the Profile, some colleges will also require completion of their own aid form. An institutional financial aid form is mailed directly back to the college and not to a processing center. In most cases, these forms are much shorter and easier to complete than the FAFSA and Profile. Each school may set their own criteria for institutional aid, thus questions may be asked concerning the family's finances that are not asked on the Federal form. I find it disconcerting that some colleges request information such as the value of IRA accounts, pension plans, the amount of life insurance on the parents, etc. This information doesn't necessarily have to impact your aid package, but it does raise the question of why they ask for this information. Unfortunately, if you don't complete their aid forms, you may not be considered for any institutional aid.

An interesting and common question on college forms is how much the family is willing to contribute towards the student's education. In my opinion, this is one of those no-win (or lose-lose) questions. If you indicate a dollar amount that is higher than what the school determines to be your expected contribution, you are creating the potential of putting some financial aid in jeopardy. If you grossly underestimate your expected contribution, they will more than likely ignore your figures. I personally would rather be ignored than take the chance of losing aid. Be conservative if you must answer this question.

THE STUDENT AID REPORT (SAR)

Approximately one-two weeks after the FAFSA is processed, the student will receive a Student Aid Report (SAR). Part of the acknowledgement section will state, based on the information submitted, whether you (the student) are eligible for a Federal Pell Grant. Don't be discouraged if you're not. Pell Grants are awarded to students with exceptional need. You may be eligible for other types of financial aid.

The SAR in essence is a scored FAFSA. It will contain all the information that was submitted when the FAFSA was filed. A facsimile of that report will be sent to the schools listed on the FAFSA.

If there are corrections that need to be made, the student can access the report at FAFSA On The Web [fafsa.ed.gov] and update the form. The student will need his or her PIN to update his or her FAFSA.

The most common correction is updating estimated tax information after the income taxes have been completed. You should not update assets unless they were stated incorrectly when the original application was completed. Assets are counted as of the date of application.

If you did estimate taxes, the following lines usually will have to be corrected (for both student and parental income):

❑   Tax Return Status-- it should change from "...will file" to "Completed."
❑   Adjusted Gross Income
❑   U.S. Taxes Paid
❑   Income Earned From Work

Keep in mind that each time a change is made to the SAR, a new SAR will be generated.

FEDERAL STUDENT AID CONTACTS

Useful Web Sites
Student Aid on the Web
www.FederalStudentAid.ed.gov
Click on Students, Parents and Counselors
At this Web site you can
• Find information on federal student aid and access publications online.
• Apply for federal student aid online using FAFSA on the Web (fafsa.ed.gov).
• Keep track of your federal student aid through the National Student Loan Data System.
College.gov
www.college.gov
This Web site is designed to motivate high school students with inspirational stories and information about planning, preparing, and paying for college.
Free Help Completing the FAFSA
www.FederalStudentAid.ed.gov/completefafsa
This Web site explains how to complete the FAFSA and the purpose of FAFSA questions.
The William D. Ford Federal Direct
Loan Program (Direct Loan)
U.S. Department of Education as lender
www.direct.ed.gov
Use this Web site to find out more information on the Direct Loan Program, such as repayment options and interactive calculators.
Direct Loan Servicing Online
www.dl.ed.gov
Use this Web site to make Direct Loan online payments, view account
balance, change billing options, enroll in electronic services, and much more.

Frequently Requested Telephone Numbers

Federal Student Aid Information Center (FSAIC)
1-800-4-FED-AID (1-800-433-3243)
TTY users can call 1-800-730-8913.
Callers in locations without access to 1-800 numbers may
call 319-337-5665 (this is not a toll-free number).
The FSAIC staff will answer your federal student aid questions
for FREE, and provide you with:
• Information about federal student aid programs,
• Help completing the FAFSA,
• Help in making corrections to your Student Aid Report (SAR),
which contains your application results,
• Information about the process of determining financial need
and awarding aid, and
• Information about your federal student loans.
You also can use an automated response system at this number to
find
out if your FAFSA has been processed and to request a copy of your
SAR.

Direct Loan Servicing
1-800-848-0979 | TTY users can call 1-800-848-0983.

Direct Loan Consolidation
1-800-557-7392 | TTY users can call 1-800-557-7395.

Studentloans.gov

Use this web site for entrance counseling, signing your Master
Promissory Note, completing your PLUS loan documents, and
managing repayment of your federal loans.

To find out if your FAFSA has been processed, simply log on to
fafsa.ed.gov and click on the link "check status of a submitted
FAFSA..."

"Let me suggest the Aid Package du Jour."

SHOPPING FOR COLLEGES

Why would anyone fish in a stream that has little or no fish in it? If you are looking for financial aid, doesn't it make sense to apply to schools that have good aid histories? In addition to looking for the right school to fit the student's academic and personal needs, make aid history another criteria in the selection process. It is no secret that some colleges have more resources than others to allocate to their students. This information can be found in financial aid publications as well as by asking each school the average percent of need they meet. "Need" is the difference between the total cost of the school and the Expected Family Contribution (EFC). Also helpful is knowing the ratio of Gift Aid (scholarships and grants) to Self-Help aid (loans and work-study). The higher the percentage of gift aid in a financial aid package, the better.

Statistics, however, can be misleading. ABC State College has a comprehensive cost of $8,000. ABC states they meet 99% of the student's need. Furthermore, you discover they have no institutional aid to offer. The reason they can meet 99% of need is due to their low cost. There just isn't that much need that can be demonstrated. Federal and state aid programs alone could result in the need being fully met. The same amount of aid applied to a private school with a cost of $40,000 would leave a huge deficit. Find the percentage of Gift Aid that comes directly from the college. Often, a school will advertise that their students received "x" amount of dollars of Gift Aid. Gift Aid includes Federal and state grants and outside scholarships, as well as institutional aid. What percent of Gift Aid is from institutional sources?

The fact that a college advertises that a high percentage of their students receive financial aid is not necessarily impressing since loans and work-study programs are considered financial aid. A college or university's average aid package is relevant only if you are the average.

FINANCIAL SAFETY SCHOOLS

Most guidance counselors suggest that students should apply to several schools, including a safety school (one that the student is virtually assured he or she will be accepted to). This is sound advice, and by following their directions, the student should have a school to attend in the fall. It also makes sense to ensure the student is applying to a school that would be affordable if the financial aid is lacking from his or her other choices. It is important to understand that regardless of a student's financial need (aid eligibility), there is no guarantee that a school will offer a financial package that will be affordable. Beyond federal and state entitlements, which often include student loans, the remaining need will be met to some extent with institutional funds. If institutional funding is lacking, the school may not be an option. Since award letters (financial aid packages) are not sent out until the early spring, inevitably what happens is some students with poor packages have to start scrambling for alternative choices. This could be problematic if the alternative school's dorms are filled or a desired curriculum is at capacity.

The solution is to apply to a financial safety school the same time as your preferred school applications are sent. A state university or community college are logical choices since their costs are significantly less that a private college or university. In many cases, the academic safety school and the financial safety school may be one and the same.

MERIT VERSUS NEED

Merit aid is based on a student's academic, athletic and/or extracurricular excellence. Need-based aid is determined by the family's financial information reflected on financial aid forms. As stated previously, the majority of merit aid a student receives comes from the college or university they are going to, not from outside sources.

There are many schools that only award institutional aid based solely on need, such as the Ivy League. Other colleges reserve most of their institutional aid for scholars and/or athletes, and there are schools that offer both need and merit aid.

The family's financial situation and the student's potential for merit money are factors that should be considered when selecting schools to apply to.

Case Scenario: Sally will graduate in the top 5% of her high school class and has exceptional SAT scores. She is applying to four Ivy League schools. None of these schools offer merit aid. In spite of her academic achievements, her financial aid will be totally need-based since these schools do not offer merit money. Her parents are disappointed that her hard work has not resulted in scholarships at these schools. They have little or no need-based aid eligibility.

Comment: First and foremost, Sally's academic achievement resulted in her being accepted at a high quality school. This accomplishment is something to be quite proud of. A financial aid solution for Sally is to apply to a good independent school that offers merit aid. At any Ivy League university, she will be one of many exceptional students. At an independent college, she would be strongly recruited and possibly could receive a full or partial scholarship.

If Sally's Expected Family Contribution had been low, chances are she would receive a large financial aid package from an Ivy League school since their aid histories are excellent.

Students who are searching for any form of merit aid should consider the type or class of school where they will be most desirable. It is often better to be a big fish in a small pond.

EVALUATING THE AWARD LETTER

The financial aid package offered to the student by the college comes in the form of an Award Letter.

Most Award Letters can be broken down into four components:

1. Estimated Cost of Attendance. The cost of attendance should include tuition, fees, room and board, books and an allowance for travel and personal expenses. The financial aid administrator at each school is responsible for calculating the student's cost of attendance based on formulas provided by law. If the total budgeted cost does not appear on an Award Letter, the student should request that information when comparing financial aid packages to other schools.

2. Family Resources (Contribution). Family resources (or family contribution) are the sum of the parent and student contribution. The Federal Need Analysis formula (based on the FAFSA) calculates Expected Family Contribution (EFC) for Federal aid. Now we are faced with how the school, based on their own policies, determines what your EFC is. Many colleges will calculate an "institutional" EFC to determine how much of their own funds they will award.

I have reviewed five Award Letters for the same student with five different institutional expected contributions. One of the college's expected contribution was $2,100 higher than any of the others. That school subtracted their expected contribution from the cost of attendance and met the remaining need. This gives an illusion of meeting 100% of the student's demonstrated need until you compare it to another school. If this practice were the norm, all that schools would have to do to claim 100% need met would be to increase the EFC to the point where they would meet the remainder.

3. Financial Aid Awards. The Financial Aid Award is a listing of the kinds and amounts of aid offered. It will include Federal, State and/or institutional aid. Financial aid includes grants, scholarships, loans and work-study programs. The different loans and programs are often confusing if this is the first time you have encountered them. It is always in your best interest to understand what is being offered to you. If any part of your Award Letter is unclear, call the school's financial aid office for clarification.

4. Acceptance/ Declination and Signature. If the family is pleased with the aid package, all that needs to be done is to sign the award letter and return it to the respective school. If the student does not want a loan or work-study, he or she may decline that part of the award. If you are dissatisfied with the aid offer, read the next section, "Appealing Your Aid Package."

Since schools are not identically priced, the total amount of the aid package is not an accurate measure for comparison. A simple formula I recommend is:

Add all Stafford and Perkins loans to any grants or scholarships. (Do not include PLUS Loans, Work-Study or any other loans made to the parents.) Subtract the sum from the total Cost of Attendance for that school. Compare this number to other schools' award packages. The school with the lowest number is the school that will cost you the least. You may then want to compare the better packages, paying special attention to the schools with high percentages of gift aid (grants or scholarships.) Incidentally, in most cases a PLUS loan is available to the parents whether or not it is included in the award letter. There are two reasons why I discount work-study when comparing award letters. First and foremost, in most cases work-study income is paid to the students as earned. It is not subtracted from your bill or credited to tuition payments. Unfortunately, this is rarely explained in the award letter and families naturally tally the financial aid, subtract it from the cost of the college and presume the balance is what they will be responsible for. Furthermore, it has been my experience that many students do not receive the hours promised after they start school, and earn much less than they anticipated, or could not work the hours because of their class schedule.

To illustrate how award letters may vary, observe the following:

SAMPLE AWARD LETTERS

	SCHOOL A	SCHOOL B	SCHOOL C
TOTAL COST:	$16,500	$18,000	$24,000
Parent Contribution	7,000	7,000	7,000
Student Contribution	1,200	1,200	1,200
Family Contribution	$ 8,200	$ 8,200	$8,200
Financial Need	$ 8,300	$ 9,800	$15,800
FINANCIAL AID:			
College Grant	$ 2,000	$ 500	$ 8,000
Stafford Loan	2,625	2,625	2,625
Work-Study *	1,200	800	1,400
Perkins Loan	800	1,000	1,200
State Aid	775	775	775
Total Award	$ 7,400	$ 5,700	$14,000

School A will cost the family $9,100 ($16,500 - $7,400), School B $12,300, and School C $10,000.

** Remember to **exclude** Work-Study when evaluating your **total** out-of-pocket cost for each school.*

APPEALING YOUR AID PACKAGE

Before discussing how to appeal an aid package, it is important to understand why some colleges are not meeting a student's financial need. As stated previously, many schools do not have the resources other schools have. Financial aid departments have a fixed amount of money to disburse and attempt to appropriate those funds to as many needy students as possible. Inevitably, these monies will run out. Also, (in defense of financial aid officers) recruiters, coaches and admissions staff often boast to prospective parents and students about how much money the school has, thus conveying a false sense of security that the financial aid department has unlimited funds. Finally, with Federal and state cutbacks and increasing college costs, colleges are either forced to dig deeper into their own pockets to meet need or they are coming up short. We may see a time when the best package isn't from the school that meets 100% of need, but from the school with the smallest aid gap.

The first principle to keep in mind is that the financial aid package awarded to an incoming freshman will most likely be his or her best package. Barring any major change in the family's financial or personal situation, the student's first year award is critical. The primary reason for this is recruitment. Colleges will do everything possible to attract a good student to their school. Once the student is enrolled, the student will most likely return the following year. I am not suggesting that in subsequent years, schools drastically cut financial aid; if this was policy, schools that made dramatic financial aid cuts to returning students would have serious retention problems. It is quite common to see returning student aid packages mirror the first year package.

Asking a financial aid officer to reevaluate an aid package is not inappropriate. Private schools are more likely to adjust their aid packages than state-supported schools. If you have a valid situation that is not reflected on the financial aid forms, such as loss of income, change of marital status, or critical health problems, contact the financial aid administrator. In most cases, they will reevaluate the financial aid. If you approach them with a "let's make a deal" attitude, you will most likely fall upon deaf ears. Unfortunately, many people are uncomfortable or embarrassed to ask for more money. Keep in mind that the worst a school can do is nothing at all. I have never heard of a college financial aid officer reducing a proposed aid package because the student or parents asked for reconsideration.

Most colleges will attempt to offer a reasonable financial aid package the first time around. If you believe that your aid is lacking, call or write the financial aid officer who prepared your package. Explain the part of your family situation that isn't covered on the financial aid form. Be able to document and substantiate what you tell them. You can tactfully make them aware if another school has offered a better package. They should also know that their school is the student's first, but not only choice. Do not substitute a PLUS loan for need-based aid when comparing aid packages.

Finally, if a school doesn't have the resources or desire to give you the financial aid that you believe you're entitled to and need, move on to another school. Don't be surprised if you get a call from School #1 in the spring with a better offer.

VERIFICATION

Verification is the process of checking the accuracy of the information submitted on the financial aid forms. Not all students go through this process and it isn't (or at least shouldn't be) a traumatic experience. Verification is only required for certain applicants, but the financial aid department may elect to verify the application information of any or all students who apply for Federal student aid. If submitted information falls out of certain norms or shows inconsistencies, your likelihood for verification increases.

The most common items verified include untaxed income, total income, number of family members in your household, number of family members attending college at least half time, and assets.

If there is considerable investment income (interest and dividends) on your tax return, and there is not a comparable amount of assets listed on the financial aid form, a red flag may be raised. For example:

Mr. Jones had $1,800 interest income on his tax return. He listed $3,500 of parental savings on his child's financial aid form. It doesn't take a rocket scientist to figure out that a lot more than $3,500 in savings would be needed to generate $1,800 of interest. If you divide $1,800 by 3 percent, you would arrive at $60,000. That is the amount of principal needed to generate $1,800 of interest. The same principle will apply to dividends, capital gains and any other income that shows up on a tax return. Perhaps the money was spent for a new car or as a down payment for a new home. As long as you can explain the discrepancy, there should be no problem.

Many colleges will ask for copies of tax returns and W-2s for routine verification checks. If a tax return has not yet been filed and a filing extension was granted, they may accept copies of Form W-2 and a copy of Form 4868, "Application for Automatic Extension of Time to File U.S. Individual Income Tax Return."

A tax return coupled with a financial aid form conveys a tremendous amount of information. There are tracks and trails everywhere on these forms. Tell the truth— it's the law. If you effectively plan for college aid, you will never have anything to hide and still be able to optimize your aid eligibility.

"Do you have any babysitting money stashed away?"

FEDERAL AID PROGRAMS

FEDERAL PELL GRANTS

A Federal Pell Grant is a grant awarded generally only to undergraduates who are attending an accredited school. For the Pell Grant Program, an undergraduate is one who has not earned a bachelor's or professional degree.

The Department of Education guarantees that each participating school receives enough money to pay the Pell Grants of its eligible students. The student's Expected Family Contribution is used to determine eligibility.

Unlike loans, grants do not have to be repaid. The current Pell Grant ranges from $555 to a maximum of $5,500 per year. Award limits for future years will depend on program funding for each year. How much the student receives depends not only on the Expected Family Contribution, but also on the cost of attendance, whether the student is full or part-time, and whether he or she will attend school for a full academic year or less.

To be eligible for a Pell Grant, the Federal Expected Family Contribution (EFC) must be less than $5,274 (2010-2011). An EFC of zero would provide for the full Pell Grant. As the EFC increases, the award decreases. The school must inform the student in writing how and when he or she will be paid and how much the award will be, and must pay the student at least once per term (semester, trimester, or quarter). The school can either credit the Pell Grant funds to the student's account, pay him or her directly, or combine these methods.

FEDERAL DIRECT STUDENT LOAN PROGRAM
AND
FEDERAL FAMILY EDUCATION LOAN PROGRAM

As of July 1st, 2010, all federal loans will be disbursed from the Federal Direct Loan program. Under the Direct Loan Program, the funds for your loan are lent to you directly by the U.S. Government. Under the FFEL Program, the funds for your loan were lent to you from a bank, credit union, or other lender that participates in the FFEL Program. Regardless of what program the school participated in, all federal student and parent loans are now under the federal Direct Loan program. New FFEL loans are not an option after July 1st, 2010, even if the student currently has loans in this program. Eligibility for a Direct student loan is determined by the college. The college also disburses the funds. A FAFSA has to be completed for a student to be considered for this loan. Once a Direct Loan is made, it is managed and collected by the U.S. Department of Education's Direct Loan Servicing Center. *Note: the Education department may contract a third-party to service this loan.*

STUDENT LOANS

Subsidized versus Unsubsidized Student Loans:

For student borrowers, Direct (Stafford) Loans are either subsidized or unsubsidized.

A subsidized loan is awarded on the basis of financial need. If you qualify for a subsidized loan, the Federal government "subsidizes" the loan by paying the interest on the loan while the borrower is in school and during the grace and deferment periods.

An unsubsidized loan is awarded if the student is not demonstrating need. If you qualify for an unsubsidized loan, interest is charged from the time the loan is disbursed until it is paid in full. You can choose to pay the interest while you're in school or allow it to accumulate. If it accumulates, it will be added to the principal amount of your loan and will increase the amount you have to repay.

Your loan from the Direct Loan program can be partially subsidized and partially unsubsidized, depending upon your aid eligibility and the amount the student is borrowing.

ANNUAL BORROWING LIMITS

The amounts shown below are the maximum yearly amounts a student can borrow in both subsidized and unsubsidized Direct Loans. However, the student can't borrow more than the cost of attendance minus any other financial aid for which he or she is eligible for. Therefore, the student may receive less than the annual maximum amounts.

Dependent Undergraduate Student:

❑ $5,500 if you're a first-year student enrolled in a program of study that is at least a full academic year. No more than $3,500 can be subsidized.

☐ $6,500 if you've completed your first year of study, and the remainder of your program is at least a full academic year. No more than $4,500 can be subsidized.

☐ $7,500 per year if you've completed two years of study (third year and beyond), and the remainder of your program is at least a full academic year. No more than $5,500 can be subsidized.

Independent Undergraduate Student:

If you're an independent undergraduate student, or a dependent student whose parents are unable to qualify for a PLUS Loan, you can borrow up to:

☐ $9,500 if you're a first-year student enrolled in a program of study that is at least a full academic year. Only $3,500 of this amount can be subsidized.

☐ $10,500 if you've completed your first year of study and the remainder of your program is at least a full academic year. Only $4,500 of this amount can be subsidized.

☐ $12,500 per year if you've completed two years of study, and the remainder of your program is at least a full academic year. Only $5,500 of this amount can be subsidized.

For periods of undergraduate study that are less than an academic year, the amounts you can borrow will be less that those listed above. The financial aid administrator at your college can tell you how much you can borrow.

Graduate Students:

☐ $20,500 each academic year.
Only $8,500 of this amount can be subsidized.

TOTAL DEBT

The total debt you can have outstanding from all Direct Loans combined is:

☐ $23,000 as a dependent undergraduate student

☐ $46,000 as an independent undergraduate student
-no more than $23,000 of this amount may be in subsidized loans

☐ $138,500 as a graduate or professional student
         -no more than $65,500 of this amount may be in subsidized loans
         -the graduate debt limit includes any Direct Stafford and FFEL Stafford Loans received for undergraduate study.

INTEREST RATES

Direct subsidized Stafford Loans have a fixed interest rate of 4.5% for loans with a first disbursement after July 1, 2010. Unsubsidized student loans have a fixed interest rate of 6.8%. For subsidized and unsubsidized loans first disbursed between July 1, 1998, and June 30, 2006, the interest rate for the period July 1, 2010, through June 30, 2011, is 2.47% for loans in repayment and 1.87% during in-school, grace, and deferment periods.

The interest rate on variable rate loans first disbursed between July 1, 1998 and June 30, 2006 is adjusted each year on July 1. You are notified of interest rate changes throughout the life of your loan.

There is a loan fee on all Direct Subsidized and Unsubsidized Loans. The loan fee is a percentage of the amount of each loan you receive. For loans first disbursed between July 1, 2010 and June 30, 2011 the loan fee is 1.0%. The loan fee will be proportionately deducted from each loan disbursement. The specific loan fee that you are charged will be reflected in a disclosure statement that is sent to you.

Additionally, if you don't make your loan payments as scheduled, you may be charged late fees and collection costs.

Repayment begins six months after the student graduates or drops below half-time. There are several repayment plans although the standard plan is amortized over ten years.

APPLYING FOR DIRECT SUBSIDIZED OR UNSUBSIDIZED STAFFORD LOANS

You will apply for and receive the loan at the school after first completing the Free Application for Federal Student Aid (FAFSA), which is used to apply for other student aid as well. Once your FAFSA is processed, your school will review the results and inform you about your loan eligibility. You must then complete the

Master Promissory Note (MPN) provided by your school. Your school should provide a link for the student (such as StudentLoans.gov) to sign the Master Promissory Note with his or her federal PIN. This is the same PIN used to sign the FAFSA. The student will also need to complete an "Entrance Interview" on the same web site. The entrance interview is a short tutorial first-year borrowers must complete that highlights the student's responsibilities when borrowing.

Under the Direct Loan Program, your lender is the U.S. Government. Your school assists the Federal government in administering the Direct Loan Program by determining your loan eligibility, processing the loan, and delivering the loan funds to you.

Your loan will be disbursed in at least two installments; no one installment can be greater than half the amount of your loan. Your loan money must first be applied to your school account to pay for tuition, room and board, fees, and other school charges. If any loan money remains, you will receive the funds by check or in cash.

If you're a first-year undergraduate student at your school, and a first-time borrower, your first payment may not be disbursed until 30 days after the first day of your enrollment period. This way, you won't have to repay the loan if you don't begin classes, or if you officially withdraw during the first 30 days of classes.

REPAYMENT OF DIRECT AND FFEL STAFFORD LOANS

After you graduate, leave school, or drop below half-time enrollment, you have a grace period of six months before you begin repayment of your Direct and FFEL Stafford Loans.

During the grace period on a subsidized loan, no interest will be charged, and you don't have to pay any of the principal. During the grace period on an unsubsidized loan, you don't have to pay any principal, but interest will be charged. You can either pay the interest or allow it to accumulate.

You will receive information about repayment and will be notified of the date repayment begins after you leave school or drop below half-time enrollment. However, you are responsible for beginning repayment on time, even if you don't receive a bill or repayment notice.

When you sign a promissory note, you are agreeing to repay the loan according to the terms of the note. The note is a binding legal document which states that, except in cases of discharge, you must repay the loan-- even if you don't complete your education, aren't able to get a job after you complete the program, or are dissatisfied with, or don't receive, the education you paid for. If you don't repay your loan on time or according to the terms in your promissory note, you may go into Default, which has very serious consequences.

You must notify the appropriate representative that manages your loan when you graduate, withdraw from school, or drop below half-time status; change your name, address, or Social Security Number, or transfer to another school. If you borrow a Direct Loan, it will be managed by the Federal Direct Loan Service Center. If you borrowed a FFEL Loan, your lender will manage it.

REPAYMENT OF DIRECT STAFFORD LOANS

Generally, you'll have from 10 to 25 years to repay your loan, depending on which repayment plan (there are several) you choose. The Direct Loan Servicing Center will notify you of the date your first payment is due. If you do not choose a repayment plan, they will place you on the Standard Repayment Plan, with fixed monthly payments for up to 10 years. Most Direct Loan borrowers choose to stay with the Standard Repayment Plan, but there are other options for borrowers who may need more time to repay or who need to make lower payments at the beginning of the repayment period. You can change repayment plans at any time by going to the Direct Loan Servicing Center's website and logging in to your account.

The Direct Loan program offers four repayment plans designed to simplify the repayment process. You may choose one of the four repayment plans:

- ☐ **The Standard Repayment Plan:** With the standard plan, you'll pay a fixed amount each month until your loans are paid in full. Your monthly payments will be at least $50, and you'll have up to 10 years to repay your loans.

Your monthly payment under the standard plan may be higher than it would be under the other plans because your loans will be repaid in the shortest time. For that reason, having a 10-year limit on repayment, you may pay the least interest.

☐ **The Income Based Repayment (IBR):** Income Based Repayment is a new repayment plan for the major types of federal loans made to students. Under IBR, the required monthly payment is capped at an amount that is intended to be affordable based on income and family size. You are eligible for IBR if the monthly repayment amount under IBR will be less than the monthly amount calculated under a 10-year standard repayment plan. If you repay under the IBR plan for 25 years and meet other requirements you may have any remaining balance of your loan(s) cancelled. Additionally, if you work in public service and have reduced loan payments through IBR, the remaining balance after ten years in a public service job could be cancelled. *To see if you qualify for IBR go to [IBRinfo.org].*

- ☐ **The Extended Repayment Plan:** Under the extended plan, you'll pay a fixed annual or graduated repayment amount over a period not to exceed 25 years. If you're a FFEL borrower, you must have more than $30,000 in outstanding FFEL Program loans. If you're a Direct Loan borrower, you must have more than $30,000 in outstanding Direct Loans. This means, for example, that if you have $35,000 in outstanding FFEL Program loans and $10,000 in outstanding Direct Loans, you can choose the extended repayment plan for your FFEL Program loans, but not for your Direct Loans. Your fixed monthly payment is lower than it would be under the Standard Plan, but you'll ultimately pay more for your loan because of the interest that accumulates during the longer repayment period.

This is a good plan if you will need to make smaller monthly payments. Because the repayment period will be 25 years, your monthly payments will be less than with the standard plan. However, you may pay more in interest because you're taking longer to repay the loans. Remember that the longer your loans are in repayment, the more interest you will pay.

- ☐ **The Graduated Repayment Plan:** With this plan, your payments start out low and increase every two years. The length of your repayment period will be up to ten years. If you expect your income to increase steadily over time, this plan may be right for you. Your monthly payment will never be less than the amount of interest that accrues between payments. Although your monthly payment will gradually increase, no single payment under this plan will be more than three times greater than any other payment.

Default

If you default, it means you failed to make payments on your student loan according to the terms of your promissory note, the binding legal document you signed at the time you took out your loan. In other words, you failed to make your loan payments as scheduled. Your school, the financial institution that made or owns your loan, your loan guarantor, and the federal government all can take action to recover the money you owe. Here are some consequences of default:

- National credit bureaus can be notified of your default, which will harm your credit rating, making it hard to buy a car or a house.
- You will be ineligible for additional federal student aid if you decide to return to school.
- Loan payments can be deducted from your paycheck.
- State and federal income tax refunds can be withheld and applied toward the amount you owe.
- You will have to pay late fees and collection costs on top of what you already owe
- You can be sued.

Discharge/Cancellation

It's possible to have your student loan debt discharged (canceled) or reduced, but only under certain specific circumstances:

- You die or are totally and permanently disabled.
- Your school closed before you could complete your program.
- For FFEL[SM] and Direct Stafford Loans only: Your school owes your lender a refund, forged your signature on a promissory note, or certified your loan even though you didn't have the ability to benefit from the coursework.
- You work in certain designated public school service professions (including teaching in a low-income school).
- You file for bankruptcy. (This cancellation is rare and occurs only if a bankruptcy court rules that repayment would cause undue hardship.)

Postponing Repayments

If you have trouble making your education loan payments, contact immediately the organization that services your loan. You might qualify for a deferment, forbearance, or other form of payment relief. It's important to take action before you are charged late fees. For Federal Perkins Loans, contact your loan servicer or the school that made you the loan. For Direct and FFEL[SM] Stafford Loans, contact your loan servicer. If you do not know who your servicer is, you can look it up in the U.S. Department of Education's National Student Loan Data System℠ [nslds.ed.gov].

Note to PLUS Loan borrowers: Generally, the eligibility requirements and procedures for requesting a deferment or forbearance for Stafford Loan borrowers also apply to you. However, since all PLUS Loans are unsubsidized, you'll be charged interest during periods of deferment or forbearance. If you don't pay the interest as it accrues, it will be capitalized (added to the principal balance of the loan), thereby increasing the amount you'll have to repay.

Deferment: You can receive a deferment for certain defined periods. A deferment is a temporary suspension of loan payments for specific situations such as reenrollment in school, unemployment, or economic hardship. You don't have to pay interest on the loan during deferment if you have a subsidized Direct or FFEL, Stafford Loan or a Federal Perkins Loan. If you have an unsubsidized Direct or FFEL Stafford Loan, you're responsible for the interest during deferment. If you don't pay the interest as it accrues (accumulates), it will be capitalized (added to the loan principal), and the amount you have to pay in the future will be higher. You have to apply for a deferment to your loan servicer (the organization that handles your loan), and you must continue to make payments until you've been notified your deferment has been granted. Otherwise, you could become delinquent or go into default.

Military Service Deferment

An active duty military deferment is available to borrowers in the Direct, FFEL, and Perkins Loan programs who are called to active duty during a war or other military operation or national emergency. This deferment is available while the borrower is serving on active duty during a war or other military operation or national emergency or performing qualifying National Guard duty during a war or other military operation or national emergency and, if the borrower was serving on or after Oct. 1, 2007, for an additional 180-day period following the demobilization date for the qualifying service.

Post-Active Duty Student Deferment

A Direct, FFEL, or Perkins Loan borrower who is a member of the National Guard or other reserve component of the U.S. Armed Forces (current or retired) and is called or ordered to active duty while enrolled at least half-time at an eligible school, or within six months of having been enrolled at least half-time, is eligible for a deferment during the 13 months following the conclusion of the active duty service, or until the borrower returns to enrolled student status on at least a half-time basis, whichever is earlier.

Economic Hardship Deferment

A Direct, FFEL, or Federal Perkins Loan borrower may qualify for an economic hardship deferment for a maximum of three years if the borrower is experiencing economic hardship according to federal regulations.

Forbearance: Forbearance is a temporary postponement or reduction of payments for a period of time because you are experiencing financial difficulty. You can receive forbearance if you're not eligible for a deferment. Unlike deferment, whether your loans are subsidized or unsubsidized, interest accrues, and you're responsible for repaying it. Your loan holder can grant forbearance in intervals of up to 12 months at a time for up to 3 years. You have to apply to your loan servicer for forbearance, and you must continue to make payments until you've been notified your forbearance has been granted.

Other Forms of Payment Relief

Although you're asked to choose a repayment plan when you first begin repayment, you might want to switch repayment plans later if a different plan would work better for your current financial situation. Under the Federal Family Education Loan Program℠, you can change repayment plans once a year. Under the Federal Direct Student Loan Program℠, you can change plans any time as long as the maximum repayment period under your new plan is longer than the time your Direct Loans have already been in repayment.

REPAYMENT INCENTIVES

Incentives are sometimes offered to students who repay their loans on time. These incentives might come in the form of interest rate rebates or reductions. For information on repayment incentives and their availability contact the Direct Loan Servicing Center (800-848-0979) for Direct Loans. If you have a FFEL, you must contact the lender.

DIRECT PARENT LOANS

(Parent Loans for Undergraduate Students)

Parents of dependent students may apply for a Direct PLUS Loan to help pay their child's education expenses as long as certain eligibility requirements are met. Graduate and professional students may apply for PLUS Loans for their own expenses.

To be eligible for a Direct PLUS Loan for Parents:

• The parent borrower must be the student's biological or adoptive parent. In some cases, the student's stepparent may be eligible.

• The student must be a dependent student who is enrolled at least half-time at a school that participates in the Direct Loan Program^{sm}. Generally, a student is considered dependent if he or she is under 24 years of age, has no dependents, and is not married, a veteran, a graduate or professional degree student, or a ward of the court.

• The parent borrower must not have an adverse credit history (a credit check will be done). If the parent does not pass the credit check, the parent may still receive a loan if someone (such as a relative or friend who is able to pass the credit check) agrees to endorse the loan. The endorser promises to repay the loan if the parent fails to do so. The parent may also still receive a loan if he or she can demonstrate extenuating circumstances.

• The student and parent must be U.S. citizens or eligible noncitizens, must not be in default on any federal education loans or owe an overpayment on a federal education grant, and must meet other general eligibility requirements for the federal student aid programs

Note: Before July 1, 2010, Stafford, PLUS, and Consolidation Loans were also made by private lenders under the Federal Family Education Loan (FFEL^{SM}) Program. As a result of recent legislation, no further loans will be made under the FFEL Program beginning July 1, 2010. Instead, all new Stafford, PLUS, and Consolidation loans will come directly from the U.S. Department of Education under the Direct Loan Program.

How does a parent get a loan?
For a Direct PLUS Loan, the parent must complete a Direct PLUS Loan Application and Master Promissory Note (MPN). The MPN is a legal document in which the borrower promises to repay the loan and any accrued interest and fees to the Department. It also explains the terms and conditions of the loan. In most cases, one MPN can be used for loans that a parent receives over multiple academic years although a separate Loan Request must be filed for each school year. If the parent previously signed an MPN to receive an FFEL PLUS loan, he or she will need to sign a new MPN for a Direct PLUS Loan.

The school's financial aid office can provide instructions on applying for a PLUS Loan and may offer the option of completing the PLUS application and MPN online at www.studentloans.gov.

How much can a parent borrow?
The annual limit on a PLUS Loan is equal to the student's cost of attendance minus any other financial aid the student receives.

For example, if the cost of attendance is $6,000 and the student receives $4,000 in other financial aid, the student's parent can request up to $2,000.

How does the parent get the loan money?
ED will send the loan funds to the student's school. In most cases, the loan will be disbursed in at least two installments, and no installment will be more than half the loan amount. The school will use the loan money first to pay the student's tuition, fees, room and board, and other school charges. If any loan funds remain, the parent will receive the amount as a check or other means, unless he or she authorizes the amount to be released to the student or transferred into the student's account at the school. Any remaining loan funds must be used for the student's education expenses.

What's the interest rate?
The interest rate is fixed at 7.9%. Interest is charged from the date of the first disbursement until the loan is paid in full.

Prior Federal Loans and Financial Aid History — Students and parents may check the interest rate, servicer information, and other financial aid history at the National Student Loan Data System [nslds.ed.gov

Interest rate cap for military members — If a parent qualifies under the Service Members Civil Relief Act, the interest rate on loans obtained before entering military service may be capped at 6% during the parent's military service. Parents must contact their loan servicer to request this benefit.

In addition, ED does not charge interest (for a period of no more than 60 months) on Direct Loans first disbursed on or after October 1, 2008, while a borrower is serving on active duty or performing qualifying National Guard duty during a war or other military operation or other emergency, and serving in an area of hostilities qualifying for special pay.

Other than interest, is there a charge to get a PLUS Loan?
The parent will pay a fee of 4% of the loan amount, deducted proportionately each time a loan disbursement is made.

When does the parent begin repaying the loan?
The repayment period for a Direct PLUS Loan begins when the loan is fully disbursed, and the first payment is due 60 days after the final disbursement. However, for Direct PLUS Loans with a first disbursement date on or after July 1, 2008, the parent may defer repayment:

• while the student on whose behalf the parent borrowed the loan is enrolled on at least a half-time basis, and

• for an additional six months after the student ceases to be enrolled at least half-time.

How does the parent pay back the loan?
The parent will repay the servicer listed on the disclosure statement provided when he or she received the loan. The loan servicer will provide regular updates on the status of the PLUS Loan, and any additional PLUS Loans that a parent receives.

Repayment Plans — The Direct PLUS Loan Program for parents offers three repayment plans-standard, extended, and graduated-that are designed to meet the different needs of individual borrowers. The terms differ between the repayment programs, but generally borrowers will have 10 to 25 years to repay a loan.

What if a parent has trouble repaying the loan?
Under certain circumstances, a borrower can receive a deferment or forbearance to temporarily stop or lower the payments on a loan.

Can the parent's PLUS Loan be transferred to the student so that it becomes the student's responsibility to repay?
No. A PLUS Loan made to the parent cannot be transferred to the student. The parent is responsible for repaying the PLUS Loan.

Can a PLUS Loan be cancelled (discharged)?
Yes, under certain conditions, such as death or total and permanent disability. A cancellation (discharge) releases the parent from all obligations to repay the loan.

CONSOLIDATION LOANS

Direct Consolidation Loans allow borrowers to combine one or more of their Federal education loans into a new loan that offers several advantages. You cannot consolidate private education loans into a federal consolidation loan.

One Lender and One Monthly Payment
With only one lender and one monthly payment due for student loans, it is easier than ever for borrowers to manage their debt. Borrowers have only one lender, the U.S. Department of Education, for all loans included in a Direct Consolidation Loan.

Flexible Repayment Options
Borrowers can choose from multiple repayment plans with various term selections to repay their consolidation loan(s), including an Income Contingent Repayment and an Income-Based Repayment Plan. These plans are designed to be flexible to meet the different and changing needs of borrowers. With a consolidation loan, borrowers can switch repayment plans at anytime. If you select the IBR Plan and want to change at a later date, your only option will be the Standard Plan.

No Minimum or Maximum Loan Amounts or Fees
There is no minimum amount required to qualify for a Direct Consolidation Loan! In addition, consolidation is *free*.

Varied Deferment Options
Borrowers with consolidation loans may qualify for renewed deferment benefits. If borrowers have exhausted the deferment options on their current Federal education loans, a consolidation loan may renew those deferment options. In addition, borrowers may be eligible for additional deferment options if they have an outstanding balance on a FFEL Program loan made before July 1, 1993, when they obtain their first Direct Loan.

Reduced Monthly Payments
A consolidation loan *may* ease the strain on a borrower's budget by lowering the borrower's overall monthly payment. The minimum monthly payment on a consolidation loan may be lower than the combined payments charged on a borrower's Federal education loans.

Retention of Subsidy Benefits

There are two (2) possible portions to a consolidation loan: Subsidized and Unsubsidized. Borrowers retain their subsidy benefits on loans that are consolidated into the subsidized portion of a consolidation loan.

Temporary In-School Consolidation Authority

During a one (1) year period, borrowers who meet certain requirements may consolidate loans that are in an in-school status into a Direct Consolidation Loan. Direct Consolidation Loans may be made under this temporary provision to borrowers whose consolidation applications are received on or after July 1, 2010 and before July 1, 2011.

Borrowers will lose the grace period on a FFEL Subsidized/Unsubsidized Stafford Loan or Direct Subsidized/Unsubsidized Loan by consolidating the loan while it is in an in-school status. Similarly, PLUS borrowers who consolidate a Federal PLUS Loan or Direct PLUS Loan that was first disbursed on or after July 1, 2008 will lose the six (6) month post-enrollment deferment period. Parent PLUS borrowers who consolidate a Federal PLUS Loan or Direct PLUS Loan that was first disbursed on or after July 1, 2008 will lose eligibility to defer repayment while the student for whom the loan was obtained is in school.

Should You Consolidate?

Are your monthly payments manageable? If you have trouble meeting your monthly payments, have exhausted your deferment and forbearance options, and/or want to avoid default, a Direct Consolidation Loan may help you.

Too many monthly payments driving you crazy? If you send payments to more than one lender every month, and want the convenience of a single monthly payment, consolidation may be right for you. With a Direct Consolidation Loan, you will have a single lender - the U.S. Department of Education - and a single monthly payment.

What are the interest rates on your loans? If you have variable interest rates on your Federal education loans, you may want to consolidate. The interest rate for a Direct Consolidation Loan is fixed for the life of the Direct Consolidation Loan. The rate is based on the weighted average interest rate of the loans being consolidated, rounded to the next nearest higher one-eighth of one percent and can not exceed 8.25 percent.

How much are you willing to pay over the long term? Like a home mortgage or a car loan, extending the years of repayment increases the total amount you have to repay.

How many payments do you have left on your loans? If you are close to paying off your student loans, it may not be worth the effort to consolidate or extend your payments.

Eligible Loans

The following federal education loans are eligible for consolidation into a Direct Consolidation Loan:

Subsidized Loans:

- Subsidized Federal Stafford Loans

- Direct Subsidized Loans

- Subsidized Federal Consolidation Loans

- Direct Subsidized Consolidation Loans

- Federal Insured Student Loans (FISL)

- Guaranteed Student Loans (GSL)

Unsubsidized Loans:

- Unsubsidized and Nonsubsidized Federal Stafford Loans

- Direct Unsubsidized Loans, including Direct Unsubsidized Loans (TEACH) (converted from TEACH Grants)

- Unsubsidized Federal Consolidation Loans

- Direct Unsubsidized Consolidation Loans

- Federal PLUS Loans (for parents or for graduate and professional students)

- Direct PLUS Loans (for parents or for graduate and professional students)

- Direct PLUS Consolidation Loans

- Federal Perkins Loans

- National Direct Student Loans (NDSL)

- National Defense Student Loans (NDSL)

- Federal Supplemental Loans for Students (SLS)

- Parent Loans for Undergraduate Students (PLUS)

- Auxiliary Loans to Assist Students (ALAS)

- Health Professions Student Loans (HPSL)

- Health Education Assistance Loans (HEAL)

- Nursing Student Loans (NSL)

- Loans for Disadvantaged Students (LDS)

How Do You Apply?

You can apply for a Direct Consolidation Loan online at [**loanconsolidation.ed.gov**] or by express phone application at **(800) 557-7392.**

DEFAULTING ON YOUR LOAN

If you default on your loan, your school, the lender or agency that holds your loan, the state, and the federal government may all take action to recover the money, including notifying national credit bureaus of your default. This affects your credit rating for a long time. For example, you may find it very difficult to borrow money from a bank to buy a car or a house.

In addition, if you default, the U.S. Department of Education might ask the Internal Revenue Service to withhold your U.S. individual income tax refund and apply it to the amount you owe or the agency holding your loan may ask your employer to deduct payments from your paycheck. Also, you are liable for expenses incurred in collecting the loan. If you decide to return to school, you're not entitled to receive any more federal student aid. Legal action might also be taken against you.

CAMPUS-BASED PROGRAMS

The Federal Supplemental Educational Opportunity Grant (FSEOG), Federal Work-Study (FWS), and Federal Perkins Loan programs are called campus-based programs because they're administered directly by the financial aid office at each participating school. Not all schools participate in all three programs. Check with your school's financial aid office to find out which programs they participate in.

How much aid you receive from each of these programs depends on your financial need, on the amount of other aid you receive, and on the availability of funds at your college or career school. Unlike the Federal Pell Grant Program, which provides funds to every eligible student, the campus-based programs provide a certain amount of funds for each participating school to administer each year. When the money for a program is gone, no more awards can be made from that program for that year. So, make sure you apply for federal student aid as early as you can. Each school sets its own deadlines for campus-based funds, and those deadlines are usually earlier than the Department of Education's deadline for filing a FAFSA.

Federal Supplemental Educational Opportunity Grants

Federal Supplemental Educational Opportunity Grants (FSEOG) are for undergraduates with exceptional financial need. Pell Grant recipients with the lowest EFCs will be the first to get FSEOGs. Just like Pell Grants, FSEOGs don't have to be paid back.

How much can I get?

You can receive between $100 and $4,000 a year, depending on when you apply, your financial need, the funding at the school you're attending, and the policies of the financial aid office at your school.

If I am eligible, how will I get the FSEOG money?

If you're eligible, your school will credit your account, pay you directly (usually by check), or combine these methods. Your school must pay you at least once per term (semester, trimester, or quarter). Schools that do not use semesters, trimesters, or quarters must disburse funds at least twice per academic year.

Federal Work-Study

Federal Work-Study (FWS) provides part-time jobs for undergraduate and graduate students with financial need, allowing them to earn money to help pay education expenses. The program encourages community service work and work related to the recipient's course of study.

Will I be paid the same as I would in any other job?

You'll be paid by the hour if you're an undergraduate. No FWS student may be paid by commission or fee. Your school must pay you directly (unless you direct otherwise) and at least monthly. Wages for the program must equal at least the current federal minimum wage but might be higher, depending on the type of work you do and the skills required. The amount you earn can't exceed your total FWS award. When assigning work hours, your employer or financial aid administrator will consider your award amount, your class schedule, and your academic progress.

What kinds of jobs are there in Federal Work-Study?

If you work on campus, you'll usually work for your school. If you work off campus, your employer will usually be a private nonprofit organization or a public agency, and the work performed must be in the public interest.

Your school might have agreements with private for-profit employers for Federal Work-Study jobs. This type of job must be relevant to your course of study (to the maximum extent possible). If you attend a career school, there might be further restrictions on the jobs you can be assigned.

Federal Perkins Loan

A Federal Perkins Loan is a low-interest (5 percent) loan for both undergraduate and graduate students with exceptional financial need. Federal Perkins Loans are made through a school's financial aid office. Your school is your lender, and the loan is made with government funds. You must repay this loan to your school.

Your school will either pay you directly (usually by check) or apply your loan to your school charges. You'll receive the loan in at least two payments during the academic year.

How much can I borrow?

You can borrow up to $5,500 for each year of undergraduate study (the total you can borrow as an undergraduate is $27,500). For graduate studies, you can borrow up to $8,000 per year (the total you can borrow as a graduate is $60,000 which includes amounts borrowed as an undergraduate). The amount you receive depends on when you apply, your financial need, and the funding level at the school.

Other than interest, is there a charge for this loan?

No, there are no other charges. However, if you skip a payment, if it's late, or if you make less than a full payment, you might have to pay a late charge plus any collection costs.

When do I pay it back?

If you're attending school at least half time, you have nine months after you graduate, leave school, or drop below half-time status before you must begin repayment. This is called "grace period." If you're attending less than half time, check with your college or career school to find out how long your grace period will be.

Additional Federal Grant Programs

Academic Competitiveness Grant

The Academic Competitiveness Grant was made available for the first time for the 2006-2007 school year for first-year college students who graduated from high school after January 1, 2006, and for second-year college students who graduated from high school after January 1, 2005.

How Much Can a Student Receive?
An Academic Competitiveness Grant provides $750 for the first year of study and $1,300 for the second year. Note: The amount of the ACG, when combined with a Pell Grant, may not exceed the student's cost of attendance. In addition, if the number of eligible students is large enough that payment of the full grant amounts would exceed the program appropriation in any fiscal year, then the amount of the grant to each eligible student may be ratably reduced.

Eligibility Requirements
To be eligible for each academic year, a student must:

- be a U.S. citizen or eligible non-citizen;
- be a Federal Pell Grant recipient;
- be enrolled at least half-time in a degree program;
- be a first or second-year undergraduate student or a student in a certificate program of at least one year in a degree program at a two-year or four-year degree-granting institution
- have completed a rigorous secondary school program of study (after January 1, 2006, if a first-year student, and after January 1, 2005, if a second-year student); and
- if a first-year student — not have been previously enrolled in an ACG-eligible program while at or below age of compulsory school attendance; or
- if a second-year student — have at least a cumulative 3.0 grade point average (GPA) on a 4.0 scale as of the end of the first year of undergraduate study.

Recognized Rigorous Secondary School Programs of Study

For qualifying for an ACG, any one of the following programs meet the "rigorous secondary school program of study" requirement:

1.   Rigorous secondary school programs designated by state education agencies (SEAs) and state-authorized local education agencies (LEAs) and recognized by the Secretary of Education.

2.   Advanced or honors secondary school programs established by states.

3.   Secondary school programs identified by a state-level partnership recognized by the State Scholars Initiative of the Western Interstate Commission for Higher Education (WICHE) of Boulder, Colorado.

4.   A program for a student who completes at least two courses in the International Baccalaureate (IB) Diploma Program with a score of four or higher on the course examinations or at least two Advanced Placement (AP) courses with a score of three or higher on the College Board's exams for those courses.

5.   A secondary school program in which a student completes, at minimum:

- Four years of English;
- Three years of math, including algebra I and a higher level class such as algebra II, geometry, or data analysis and statistics;
- Three years of science, including one year each of at least two of the following courses: biology, chemistry, and physics;
- Three years of social studies; and
- One year of a language other than English.

For each calendar year, the Secretary publishes a list of all rigorous secondary school programs of study.

National Smart Grant

The National Science and Mathematics Access to Retain Talent Grant, also known as the National Smart Grant is available during the third and fourth years of undergraduate study (or fifth year of a five-year program) to at least half-time students who are eligible for the Federal Pell Grant and who are majoring in physical, life, or computer sciences, mathematics, technology, engineering or a critical foreign language; or non-major single liberal arts programs. The student must also be enrolled in the courses necessary to complete the degree program and to fulfill the requirements of the intended eligible major in addition to maintaining a cumulative grade point average (GPA) of at least 3.0 in course work required for the major. The National SMART Grant award is in addition to the student's Pell Grant award.

How Much Can A Student Receive?

A National SMART Grant will provide up to $4,000 for each of the third and fourth years of undergraduate study. The amount of the SMART Grant, when combined with a Pell Grant, may not exceed the student's cost of attendance. In addition, if the number of eligible students is large enough that payment of the full grant amounts would exceed the program appropriation in any fiscal year, then the amount of the grant to each eligible student may be ratably reduced.

Eligible Students

- be a U.S. citizen or eligible non-citizen;
- be Pell Grant-eligible during the same award year;
- be enrolled at least half-time;
- be in the third or fourth year of an undergraduate degree program (or fifth year of a five-year program);
- be pursuing a major in physical, life, or computer sciences, mathematics, technology, engineering or a critical foreign language; or non-major single liberal arts programs, and
- have at least a 3.0 GPA on a 4.0 scale as of the end of the second award year and continue to maintain a 3.0 GPA that must be checked prior to the beginning of each payment period (e.g., semester).

Note - A student is eligible to receive a National SMART Grant if the student enrolls in the courses necessary to complete the degree program and to fulfill the requirements of the intended eligible major.

That is, an otherwise eligible student can receive a National SMART Grant for a payment period only if the student is enrolled in at least one course that meets the specific requirements of the student's National SMART Grant-eligible major and it is not necessary that the course be offered by the academic department that confers the degree in the eligible major. For example, a student majoring in biology is eligible to receive a National SMART Grant during a semester in which he or she is enrolled in a physics course if the physics course is required for the major even if the student is not enrolled in any biology courses.

A student who is taking general education courses or electives that satisfy general degree requirements for the student's National SMART Grant-eligible program, but who is not taking at least one course specific to and required for the National SMART Grant-eligible major, is not eligible for a National SMART Grant payment for that payment period. For example, the biology student described above may be taking courses during a semester in the humanities, the arts, and physical education in order to fulfill the general education requirements of the degree program or major. However, to be eligible for a National SMART Grant the student must also be enrolled in at least one course required for the student's National SMART Grant major. If the student were enrolled only in courses that satisfy the general education requirements of the National SMART Grant-eligible program, but not in any courses that are specific to the major, he or she would not be eligible for a National SMART Grant payment for the semester.

For a list or eligible fields of study, go to:[http://ifap.ed.gov/dpcletters/attachments/GEN1012Attach.pdf}

TEACH Grant

Through the College Cost Reduction and Access Act of 2007, Congress created the Teacher Education Assistance for College and Higher Education (TEACH) Grant Program that provides grants of up to $4,000 per year to students who intend to teach in a public or private elementary or secondary school that serves students from low-income families. If, after reading all of the information on this fact sheet, you are interested in learning more about the TEACH Grant Program, you should contact the financial aid office at the college where you will be enrolled.

Conditions
In exchange for receiving a TEACH Grant, you must agree to serve as a
full-time teacher in a high-need field in a public or private elementary or secondary school that serves low-income students (see below for more information on high-need fields and schools serving

low-income students). As a recipient of a TEACH Grant, you must teach for at least four academic years within eight calendar years of completing the program of study for which you received a TEACH Grant. IMPORTANT: If you fail to complete this service obligation, all amounts of TEACH Grants that you received will be converted to a Federal Direct Unsubsidized Stafford Loan. You must then repay this loan to the U.S. Department of Education. You will be charged interest from the date the grant(s) was disbursed. Note: TEACH Grant recipients will be given a 6-month grace period prior to entering repayment if a TEACH Grant is converted to a Direct Unsubsidized Loan.

Student Eligibility Requirements
To receive a TEACH Grant you must meet the following criteria:

- Complete the Free Application for Federal Student Aid (FAFSA℠), although you do not have to demonstrate financial need.
- Be a U.S. citizen or eligible non-citizen.
- Be enrolled as an undergraduate, post-baccalaureate, or graduate student in a postsecondary educational institution that has chosen to participate in the TEACH Grant Program.
- Be enrolled in course work that is necessary to begin a career in teaching or plan to complete such course work. Such course work may include subject area courses (e.g., math courses for a student who intends to be a math teacher).
- Meet certain academic achievement requirements (generally, scoring above the 75th percentile on a college admissions test or maintaining a cumulative GPA of at least 3.25).
- Sign a TEACH Grant Agreement to Serve (see below for more information on the TEACH Grant Agreement to Serve).

High-Need Field
High-need fields are the specific areas identified below:

- Bilingual Education and English Language Acquisition.
- Foreign Language.
- Mathematics.
- Reading Specialist.
- Science.
- Special Education.

- Other identified teacher shortage areas as of the time you begin teaching in that field. These are teacher subject shortage areas (not geographic areas) that are listed in the Department of Educations Annual Teacher Shortage Area Nationwide Listing.

As of July 1, 2010, a recipient of an initial TEACH Grant who has received an academic degree, or expertise, in a field that was, at the time the recipient signed the TEACH Grant Agreement to Serve, designated as high-need, but no longer has that designation, can fulfill the service obligation associated with the TEACH Grant by teaching in that high-need field.

Schools Serving Low-Income Students
Schools serving low-income students include any elementary or secondary school that is listed in the Department of Educations Annual Directory of Designated Low-Income Schools for Teacher Cancellation Benefits. To access the Directory, please go to https://www.tcli.ed.gov/CBSWebApp/tcli/TCLIPubSchoolSearch.jsp.

TEACH Grant Agreement to Serve
Each year you receive a TEACH Grant, you must sign a TEACH Grant Agreement to Serve that is available electronically on the TEACH Grant ability to serve Web site. The TEACH Grant Agreement to Serve specifies the conditions under which the grant will be awarded, the teaching service requirements, and includes an acknowledgment by you that you understand that if you do not meet the teaching service requirements you must repay the grant as a Federal Direct Unsubsidized Loan, with interest accrued from the date the grant funds were disbursed. Specifically, the TEACH Grant Agreement to Serve will require the following:

- For each TEACH Grant-eligible program for which you received TEACH Grant funds, you must serve as a full-time teacher for a total of at least four academic years within eight calendar years after you completed or withdrew from the academic program for which you received the TEACH Grant.
- You must perform the teaching service as a highly-qualified teacher at a low-income school. The term highly-qualified teacher is defined in section 9101(23) of the Elementary and Secondary

Education Act of 1965 or in section 602(10) of the Individuals With Disabilities Education Act.

- Your teaching service must be in a high-need field.
- You must comply with any other requirements that the Department of Education determines to be necessary.
- If you do not complete the required teaching service obligation, TEACH Grant funds you received will be converted to a Federal Direct Unsubsidized Stafford Loan that you must repay, with interest charged from the date of each TEACH Grant disbursement.

IMPORTANT REMINDER
If you receive a TEACH Grant but do not complete the required teaching service, as explained above, you will be required to repay the grants as a Federal Direct Unsubsidized Stafford Loan, with interest charged from the date of each TEACH Grant disbursement.

Next Steps
If you are interested in learning more about the TEACH Grant Program, you should contact the financial aid office at the college where you will be enrolled to find out if they will participate in the TEACH Grant Program.

CHAPTER
SIX

IN SEARCH OF MORE MONEY

FINANCING THE NON-NEED PORTION OF COLLEGE COSTS

Unless your family has virtually no income and assets, you will be responsible for a portion of the total cost of college. Income and/or assets are considered viable sources of funds. In most instances, the Expected Family Contribution is the minimum amount of money that will be contributed with out-of-pocket funds, not necessarily what you will pay. Before you run to the bank, consider the future financial aid and tax consequences of how much you borrow and where you borrow from.

Student Savings

If there are any assets in the student's name, they should be expended first. As discussed earlier in this book, assets in the student's name at time of application will result in a 20% assessment of their total savings and investments. There are situations where it is not possible to shelter or reposition student assets. If this is the case, using the student's money first will ensure that their remaining assets will not be reassessed at 20% the following year.

Student and Parental Income

Any monies that can be budgeted from income for college expenses will be money that you will not be borrowing and paying interest on. Make an objective of saving $100, $200, etc. every month, specifically to help offset college costs. Two hundred dollars monthly from earnings will decrease the student or parent's debt load by $9,600 in four years (before interest)!

Parental Savings

Money that is not sheltered in pension-type funds should be liquid and is a good source of capital to help offset college costs. If possible, maintain an emergency fund (at least six months of fixed expenses) in liquid savings for non-college expenditures.

Parental Investments

If the family owns stocks, bonds, mutual funds, etc., they can be liquidated to offset non-need costs. Keep in mind that if you are going to incur large capital gains at sale (in addition to the income tax liability), your income will increase, thus your Expected Family Contribution for the following year will also increase. This same situation occurs when parents withdraw IRA's and pension monies to pay for college. They incur a substantial tax liability as well as a higher EFC because their taxable income has increased. The opposite effect occurs when you have a capital loss. Your tax liability decreases and your EFC decreases. If your investments are your source of college funding and you anticipate large capital gains, consider selling them prior to January 1 of the student's junior year in high school to avoid an income increase in the tax year that will impact aid eligibility.

HOME EQUITY

Home equity can be an excellent source of money for college funding. When interest rates are low, it is common for home equity loans to be significantly less expensive than other federal fixed rate loans. In most cases, the interest paid on a home equity loan will be tax-deductible.

Borrowing against your home does not increase the student's aid eligibility for federal aid because the equity in the parent's primary home is excluded as an assessable asset. However, some colleges will treat home equity as an asset when determining how much institutional aid they may offer. Deciding what loan is more cost-effective should be determined by comparing current interest rates, the tax consequences of each loan, the costs of procuring the loan, and, as previously mentioned, whether home equity is impacting institutional aid.

Home Equity Loan versus Line of Credit

If you are contemplating borrowing from the equity of your home to help pay college costs and don't know whether to take out a lump sum all at once, or establish a home equity line of credit, consider the following:

If you borrow from a home equity loan, you will receive a lump sum of money that you will have to "park" until your tuition bills come due each year. While that money is earning a nominal amount of interest, you will be paying significantly more on the loan. Banks make money by establishing a spread between what they pay and what they charge By establishing a line of credit, you only have to borrow money as needed, so your payments will be smaller and you will pay less interest. If you think that you would need $20,000 for the next four years ($5,000 x 4), establish a $20,000 credit line now. This will save you from going back to the bank each year to reapply for a new loan. Remember, with a credit line, your monthly payments are based on what you actually owe. The only drawback to a line of credit is you will have a variable loan rate. This could result in larger payments if interest rates rise. As long as you itemize your deductions at tax time, your interest payments on either loan should be deductible.

PLUS Loans

The Federal PLUS Loan enables parents to borrow up to the cost of education minus any financial aid received. Although the loan amounts are attractive, you always have to consider the consequences of borrowing large sums of money.

PLUS Loans have a fixed interest rate of 7.9% for loans with a first disbursement after July 1, 2006. Interest is charged on the loan from the date the first disbursement is made until the loan is paid in full. The loan is disbursed in at least two parts and payments generally begin 60 days after the last disbursement.

Eligibility for a PLUS Loan is determined by a credit check. In most cases parents will not be denied unless they have an adverse credit history – defined as being more than 90 days late on a loan payment. The PLUS Loan is in the parents' name not the student. Even though parents may have an arrangement with the student to pay back the loan, the legal responsibility remains with the parent. A parent can not give or release the PLUS loan to the student.

Installment Plans

Many colleges offer programs that allow parents to spread tuition payments over a ten to twelve month period rather than paying a lump sum at the beginning of each semester. Most of these programs charge no interest but will have a nominal fee to enroll in the plan. Check with your college to see what type of extended payment plans are offered and look closely at the terms. Most installment plans are very legitimate and cost-effective. Since there is no interest charged on the majority of these loans, you can save some interest by enrolling in an installment plan at the school and making your monthly payments via a home equity loan.

Retirement

Borrowing from, or withdrawal from your retirement plan is the last place I would recommend to fund college expenses. Loans will be treated as a taxable distribution if for any reason you become unemployed and can not immediately pay back the total loan balance. If you subscribe to the myth that you're paying yourself interest, what you are not seeing is the potential growth your money is losing by being out of the plan. Distributions from retirement accounts will be taxable and increase your income. The next year a financial aid form is completed your inflated income will decrease the student's aid eligibility. Finally, subscribe to the notion that there is life after our children are independent of us. Your retirement nest egg will make life a little sweeter.

The Two-Plus-Two Alternative

There are many middle-income families with little or no disposable income, high consumer debt, little home equity and an Expected Family Contribution higher than they can afford. Rather than amass even more debt through PLUS Loans, etc., consider a community college for your child's first two years. These schools are often underrated; but in fact could provide an excellent base for your student to transfer from. Many schools offer two-plus-two programs that guarantee immediate acceptance upon the successful completion of the first two years. An average student who does well at a two-year school will often find it much easier to be accepted at a four-year school as a transfer student than as a prospective freshman. Incidentally, I have never seen a diploma from a four-year college or university that had an asterisk on it denoting the student was a transfer!

JUSTIFYING COLLEGE COSTS

Each year I see many parents whose children want to go to a college that would create a significant financial drain and hardship to the family. In some of these cases, I question the costs and benefits of the student's school choices. Certain situations such as a unique curriculum or being part of a prestigious department, or renowned university may warrant a financial burden to the family. However, does it make sense for a student or family to generate an additional fifty or a hundred thousand dollars of loans over four years if the student is entering as a liberal arts major or is undeclared? Will an elementary education major have more job opportunities graduating from a private college that a state university? Will the pay differential justify the increase in college costs? How relevant is class size? It is not uncommon for state universities to have certain core courses in a large class format, but what percentage of the student's classes over four years will be in a lecture hall? Is the student going to get lost in a huge university or will he or she just be one of many microcosms on a larger campus? Would it make sense to contain the undergraduate debt and spend a year at a prestigious university pursuing a Masters degree?

In certain cases, additional expense and financial sacrifice are well justified. It is also logical to ask some of the questions I have presented to arrive at an informed decision.

As parents, most of us want to do everything we can for our children. However, common sense and reality cannot be ignored when evaluating our capacity to pay for their education.

Military Scholarships

Military scholarships are awarded on the basis of merit rather than financial need. The Army, Marine, Air Force and Naval Reserve Officer Training Corps (ROTC) are awarded at hundreds of colleges throughout the United States. Scholarships can include free tuition, room and board as well as a tax-free monthly stipend. These scholarships are based strictly on merit. Upon completion of college, the student will have a specific time commitment that he or she must serve in the armed forces.

Visit www.todaysmilitary .com for more information.

ALTERNATIVE LOANS FOR UNDERGRADUATE STUDENTS

Alternative (private) loans are non-federal loans that allow the student (often cosigned by the parent) the opportunity to borrow funds needed to fill in their financial aid gap. Private education loans can be used for any school related expense - including books, tuition, supplies, lab fees, transportation and housing expenses. Most alternative loans are deferred until the student has left college. However, interest on alternative loans is continually accruing, thus increasing the loan balance. Private loans are usually more expensive than federal loans and do not offer many benefits that federal loans have, so pursue federal loans first, then, if necessary, apply for alternative loans. You cannot consolidate your private loans into a federal consolidation loan.

Interest rates for private loans are usually variable and are tied into an index such as Prime or LIBOR plus a certain percentage based on your credit. Many lenders offer loans without fees, but published rates and/or fees may be considerably different depending on credit history. Furthermore interest rates may be lower during deferment than they are when you are repaying the loan. Private education loans are normally applied for on-line . In most cases, you will not know what rate the lender will charge you until you apply for the loan and the lender does a credit check. This makes the loan comparison process more cumbersome. Before you commit to a lender, apply to two or three of them and compare the rates and fees.

*"Have I got a deal for **You**!"*

SCHOLARSHIP SEARCH SERVICES

With all the legitimate expenses associated with college, a scholarship search service is one to avoid. Don't be lured by such advertising as, "Guaranteed Available Sources" or, "Money-Back Guarantee." Be wary of scams with time-sensitive response times or "lines" such as "You've been selected by a "national foundation' to receive a scholarship or "you're a finalist" in a contest you never entered. What most of these services actually provide is a printed list of scholarships or financial aid sources that the student could be eligible for. Another gimmick involves mass-mailing postcards urging parent's to reserve their place at a financial aid meeting by calling a specified number with their registration code. These often high-pressured "seminars" generally offer little or no value and are motivated primarily to "sign you up" for their services. Keep in mind the old adage, "If something sounds too good to be true, it probably is." Information on legitimate, attainable private scholarships can be found in the high school guidance office or from the admissions or financial aid office at the college the student is applying to.

The simplest way to search scholarships is via the internet. One of the most comprehensive sites I have seen is FastWEB (fastweb.com). The scholarship search is free and updates the student when new sources become available. Keep in mind that positive results from search services are infrequent at best.

You may also inquire whether your employer or local civic organizations offer scholarships. Remember, the overwhelming amount of scholarship money a student receives will come from the college or university they attend, not from outside sources.

THE COLLEGE FINANCIAL AID CONSULTANT

First and foremost, financial aid consultants are not scholarship search services. In my opinion, the negative press these services receive is often well-deserved. A financial aid consultant's role is to guide the family through the financial aid process. If you find their primary objective is to sell products or suggest tactics that are unethical or illegal, walk away. Be cautious if you receive a "time-sensitive" mailing or if you receive an invitation where you have to provide a code from the letter to be able to register.

The need and importance for a legitimate and competent financial aid specialist can be demonstrated by the phrase "financial aid perspective." Case in point: Mrs. Brown, the financial aid administrator at a local independent college, has a reputation for doing everything possible to help students attend her school. Unfortunately, she does not have an unlimited budget and must stretch the grant money out as far as possible. Although Mrs. Brown's sincerity is beyond reproach, there are two inherent perspective problems. First and foremost, the college, not the student, employs Mrs. Brown. Within her means, she will be accommodating, but her means may be limited and she may be dealing with hundreds, if not thousands of students. Second, despite Mrs. Brown's dedication, will she suggest applying to other schools? To what degree will she discuss appealing the financial aid package, or will she offer suggestions that may increase financial aid eligibility, knowing that her school doesn't have the means to meet the student's increased need?

A financial aid consultant works for you. He or she has no vested interest in any particular school, governmental agency or lending institution. The consultant is employed to help the family receive the best financial aid package legally possible and has only one vested interest— the client. The end result may be a substantial reduction in expenses each year. This is accomplished by having a thorough understanding of the financial aid process and employing sound college financial aid planning principles. This is analogous to tax preparers suggesting tax reduction strategies to their clients. Keep in mind that most financial planners or tax preparers have little or no experience with financial aid. What is also true is the fact that most college financial aid officers are not financial planners.

A financial aid consultant needs to be a good financial planner. In addition to a strong financial aid background, he or she should have the competence to address issues such as how to effectively pay for the portion of college costs not subsidized by financial aid. Expertise in taxation, investments, and retirement plans can be critical in recommending a cost-effective plan to fund an education. Poor choices in college funding not only will cost you more money, but also has the potential to negatively impact future financial aid. Finding a planner with this unique blend of skills may make the difference in whether or not the student can attend his or her school of choice.

Knowledge is power. With college costs families are faced with, you need all the help you can get.

EDUCATION TAX INCENTIVES

(Education tax credits and deductions often change to some degree each year. Refer to IRS publication 970 or your current year Form 1040 instructions to ensure you have the most up-to-datet tax information.)

Qualified Education Expenses:
For purposes of the education credits and deductions, qualified education expenses are tuition and certain related expenses required for enrollment or attendance at an eligible educational institution. Student-activity fees are included in education expenses only if the fees must be paid to the institution as a condition of enrollment or attendance. However, expenses for books, supplies, and equipment required for a course of study are included in qualified education expenses whether or not the materials are purchased from the educational institution.

Money distributed from qualified tuition programs (529 plans) can also use the money for room and board, as long as the beneficiary is at least a half-time student. The full cost of room and board counts if the student's housing is owned or operated by the college. Off-campus housing costs can qualify up to the allowance for room and board that the college includes in its cost of attendance for federal financial-aid purposes (your college financial-aid office can give you that figure).

THE HOPE SCHOLARSHIP CREDIT

2009 and 2010 Changes

For tax years 2009 and 2010, the following changes have been made to the Hope credit. The modified credit is now referred to as the American Opportunity Tax Credit (AOC).

- The maximum amount of the AOC increases to $2,500 per student. The credit is phased out (gradually reduced) if your modified adjusted gross income (AGI) is between $80,000 and $90,000 ($160,000 and $180,000 if you file a joint return). *Exception.* For 2009, if you claim a Hope credit for a student who attended a school in a Midwestern disaster area, you can choose to figure the amount of the credit using the previous rules. However, you must use the previous rules in figuring the credit for all students for which you claim the credit. For 2009, the amount of your Hope credit is phased out (gradually reduced) if your modified adjusted gross income (AGI) is between $50,000 and $60,000 ($100,000 and $120,000 if you file a joint return). You cannot claim a Hope credit if your modified AGI is $60,000 or more ($120,000 or more if you file a joint return).

- The AOC can now be claimed for the first four years of post-secondary education. Previously the credit could be claimed for only the first two years of post-secondary education.

- Generally, 40% of the AOC is now a refundable credit, which means that you can receive up to $1,000 even if you owe no taxes. However, none of the credit is refundable if the taxpayer claiming the credit is a child (a) who is under age 18 (or a student who is at least age 18 and under age 24 and whose earned income does not exceed one-half of his or her own support), (b) who has at least one living parent, and (c) who does not file a joint return.

- The term "qualified tuition and related expenses" has been expanded to include expenditures for "course materials." For this purpose, the term "course materials" means books, supplies, and equipment needed for a course of study whether or not the materials are purchased from the educational institution as a condition of enrollment or attendance.

A parent can only claim the credit if they claim the child as a dependent on their tax return. You cannot claim this credit if you filing status is *Married Filing Separately*.

Use IRS Form 8863 to apply for this credit.

THE LIFETIME LEARNING CREDIT

The Lifetime Learning Credit may be claimed for the qualified tuition and related expenses of the students in the taxpayer's family (i.e., the taxpayer, the taxpayer's spouse, or an eligible dependent) who are enrolled in eligible educational institutions. The credit amount is equal to 20 percent of the taxpayer's first $10,000 of out-of-pocket qualified tuition and related expenses. Thus, the maximum credit a taxpayer may claim for a taxable year is $2,000. These amounts are not indexed for inflation.

If the taxpayer is claiming a Hope Scholarship Credit (AOC) for a particular student, none of that student's expenses for that year may be applied toward the Lifetime Learning Credit. The amount a taxpayer may claim for the Lifetime Learning Credit is gradually reduced for taxpayers who have modified adjusted gross income between $50,000 ($100,000 for married taxpayers filing jointly) and $60,000 ($120,000 for married taxpayers filing jointly). The modified adjusted gross income limitation will be indexed for inflation in 2006 and years thereafter. The definition of modified adjusted gross income is the same as it is for purposes of the Hope Scholarship Credit.

Unlike the Hope Scholarship Credit, there is no limit to the number of years in which a Lifetime Learning Credit may be claimed for each student. This credit is available for all years of postsecondary education and for courses to acquire or improve job skills. The student does not need to be pursuing a degree or other recognized education credential to receive this credit. A parent can only claim the credit if they claim the child as a dependent on their tax return.

A parent can only claim the credit if they claim the child as a dependent on their tax return. You cannot claim this credit if you filing status is *Married Filing Separately*.

Use IRS Form 8863 to apply for this credit.

STUDENT LOAN INTEREST DEDUCTION

Taxpayers who have taken loans to pay the cost of attending an eligible educational institution for themselves, their spouse, or their dependent generally may deduct interest they pay on these student loans. The IRS Form 1098-E is used to report to you the amount of interest you have paid on student or parent loans during a single calendar year. The maximum deduction each taxpayer is permitted to take is $2,500. The AGI limit for the full interest deduction is $50,000 for single filers, phasing out at a maximum of $65,000. For joint filers, the phase-out begins at $105,000 to a maximum of $135,000.

The student loan interest deduction is an above-the-line deduction. This means you do not have to itemize (Schedule A) to claim this deduction. This becomes quite beneficial to recent college graduates who use the standard deduction on their tax return.

You generally can claim the deduction in any tax year in which:

✓ Your filing status is anything other than married filing a separate return

✓ No one else is claiming an exemption for you on his or her tax return.

✓ You are legally obligated to pay the interest on a qualified student loan.

✓ You paid interest on a qualified student loan.

DEDUCTION FOR HIGHER EDUCATION EXPENSES

The EGRRA created an above-the-line deduction for qualified tuition and related expenses. The deduction particularly benefits taxpayers whose income exceeds the eligibility threshold for the Hope Scholarship and Lifetime Learning tax credits. The tuition and fees deduction can reduce amount of your income subject to tax by up to $4,000.

This deduction is taken as an adjustment to income. This means you can claim this deduction even if you do not itemize deductions on Schedule A (Form 1040). This deduction may be beneficial to you if you do not qualify for the American Opportunity, Hope, or Lifetime learning credits.

Married taxpayers filing jointly could deduct up to $4,000 if their AGI is less than $130,000 and $2,000 if their AGI is less than $160,000. The income limits for single taxpayers or head of household is $65,000 (up to $4,000) and $80,000 (up to $2,000). You do not need to itemize to claim this deduction.

529 PLANS (QUALIFIED TUITION PLANS)

There are two types of 529 plans:

The Prepayment Plan allows people to prepay all or part of a designated beneficiary's qualified higher education expenses, usually limited to tuition. These plans give the parents the opportunity to buy shares or units of college tuition that are guaranteed to grow at the same rate as college tuition. The prepayment plan had not shared the same popularity as the savings plan and had significant aid detriments discussed in the financial aid implications section of this book.

The Savings Plan (state-sponsored plans), allows people to make contributions to a special account established for the purpose of accumulating earnings that can later be withdrawn to pay a designated beneficiary's qualified higher education expenses. All states offer these plans with various investment options. Either type of 529 plan allows a person to make deposits of funds (not securities or other assets) for the purpose of obtaining tax-free growth of earnings when the funds are withdrawn to pay for qualified higher education expenses of a designated beneficiary.

For 529 plans, federal law defines qualified higher education expenses to be charges for tuition, fees, room and board, books, supplies, and equipment required for enrollment or attendance at an "eligible educational institution." An "eligible educational institution" is a college, community college, university, or a professional school (such as law school, veterinary school, or medical school). For purposes of 529 plans, eligible educational institutions do not include elementary or secondary schools.

529 savings plans are excellent savings vehicles for education. They are offered in all states including the District of Columbia. Many states offer a full or partial state income tax deduction. In most cases, these plans are setup with the parent or grandparent as the owner and the student as the beneficiary. Should the beneficiary not attend school, the owner can name another beneficiary and maintain their tax-free growth.

When investing into a 529 savings plan you should consider the time frame the money is going to be in the plan for. When will you need to start to withdrawing money from the plan? A general financial planning principle is the shorter the time horizon, the more conservative your investment selection should be. What is it going to cost you to invest in the plan? Some plans higher very high fees and sales charges. These expenses will have an impact on the growth of your investment. If you live in a state that offers a tax deduction, consider that plan first before utilizing another state's plan.

Transferring Custodial Accounts to 529 Plans

Monies held in Uniform Gift to Minors Act (UGMA) or Uniform Transfer to Minors Act (UGTA) may be transferred into a 529 plan. However, you will not be able to change the beneficiary on this account, and once the minor reaches the age of majority, he or she will assume direct ownership. Though money transferred from an UGMA to a 529 savings plan is still technically the child's asset, it will no longer be considered a student asset for the purposes of financial aid and is reported on the FAFSA for dependent students as a parental asset. Keep in mind that securities cannot be transferred into 529 plans, the custodial account will need to be sold first. This will create a taxable event that may incur capital gains. This can have an impact on the student's aid eligibility.

Gift and Estate Taxes

A parent or grandparent has the opportunity to gift up to $13,000 a year or by making an election on a gift tax return (Form 709) to frontload five years ($65,000) without paying gift tax. The advantage of this is the owner still maintains control of the account and, if necessary, could take the money back and then include it back into their taxable estate. Furthermore, for financial aid purposes monies owned by grandparents in 529 plans currently are not considered assets when determining federal financial aid eligibility.

COVERDELL ESAS
(formerly Education IRA's)

You may be able to contribute to a Coverdell Education Savings Account (ESA) to finance a beneficiary's qualified education expenses. The contribution is NOT deductible. Contributions to 529 plans are fully or partially deductible in many states.

A Coverdell ESA is a trust or custodial account set up in the United States solely for the purpose of paying qualified education expenses for the designated beneficiary of the account. Qualified higher education expenses include expenses for tuition, fees, books, supplies, and equipment required for enrollment or attendance. If the designated beneficiary is enrolled at least half time at an eligible educational institution, certain room and board expenses are qualified education expenses. Expenses also include amounts contributed to a qualified tuition program for the same designated beneficiary. Qualified expenses include public, private and religious elementary and secondary school expenses.

The designated beneficiary must be under the age of 18 when the account is established. Any balance in a Coverdell ESA must be distributed within 30 days after the date the beneficiary reaches age 30. These age limits do not apply to beneficiaries with special needs.

There is no limit to the number of Coverdell ESAs that can be established for one beneficiary. However, total contributions made to all Coverdell ESAs for any beneficiary in one tax year cannot be greater than $2,000.

In general, the designated beneficiary of a Coverdell ESA can receive tax free distributions to pay qualified education expenses. The distributions are tax free to the extent the amount of the distributions do not exceed the beneficiary's qualified education expenses. If a distribution does exceed the beneficiary's qualified education expenses, a portion of the distribution is taxable. For information on how to determine the part of any distribution that is taxable earnings, refer to Publication 970, *Tax Benefits for Education*.

Financial Aid Implications

As of July 1, 2006, Coverdell Education Savings Accounts, 529 College Savings Plans, and 529 Prepaid Tuition Plans will receive equal treatment in the calculation of federal financial aid eligibility. Specifically, money in these accounts will be regarded as assets of the parent if the parent is the owner of the account, rather than the student, and thereby displace a smaller amount of financial aid. If you are a dependent student who owns qualified educational benefits or education savings accounts, such as Coverdell Savings Accounts, 529 College Savings Plans, or the refund value of 529 prepaid tuition plans, you report the values with your parents' asset information. This is far better than a UGMA or UTMA account where the student is the owner, and the assets are assessed at a much higher rate.

Distributions from Coverdell Education Savings Accounts and 529 College Savings Plans that are not subject to federal income tax are not counted as parent or student income in the determination of federal financial aid eligibility. Distributions for qualified educational expenses therefore do not reduce financial aid eligibility.

Education Savings Bonds

The savings bond education tax exclusion allows qualified taxpayers to exclude from their gross income all or part of the interest paid upon the redemption of eligible Series EE savings bonds and Series I savings bonds issued after 1989, when the bond owner pays qualified higher education expenses at eligible institutions.

You must have been at least 24 years old when you purchased the bonds, and for dependent students, the bonds must be registered in the parent's name, not the student's. Bonds must be redeemed in the year the education expenses occurred and qualified education expenses are limited to tuition and tuition-related fees – not room and board.

This tax exclusion is reduced or eliminated at specific income limits depending on your filing status. Instructions and limits are found on IRS Form 8815.

USING IRA WITHDRAWALS TO PAY HIGHER EDUCATION EXPENSES

A taxpayer may make withdrawals from a Traditional Individual Retirement Account (IRA) to pay the qualified higher education expenses for the taxpayer, the taxpayer's spouse, or the child or grandchild of the taxpayer or taxpayer's spouse at an eligible educational institution. The taxpayer will owe federal income tax on the amount withdrawn, but will not be subject to the 10 percent early withdrawal tax that applies when amounts are withdrawn from an individual retirement account before the account holder reaches age 59 1/2. Although this incentive removes the 10% penalty, it will add the amount of your withdrawal to your taxable income. An increase in income may negatively impact future financial aid eligibility. Withdrawals from a Roth IRA used to pay for qualified education expenses are tax free.

Author's Choice of Best Schools for Financial Aid

The following colleges and universities have been selected to the Author's "Best Schools For Financial Aid" list. Each edition of this text has additions and deletions to this list due to fiscal changes from school to school. The fact that a specific college or university is not on this list does not suggest a student will not or can not receive an excellent financial aid package from that institution.

California

California Institute of Technology	Pasadena
Chapman University	Orange
Claremont McKenna College	Claremont
Harvey Mudd College	Claremont
Occidental College	Los Angeles
Pitzer College	Claremont
Pomona College	Claremont
Scripps College	Claremont
Stanford University	Stanford
University of Southern California	Los Angeles

Colorado

University of Northern Colorado	Greeley

Connecticut

Connecticut College	New London
Trinity College	Hartford
Wesleyan University	Middletown
Yale University	New Haven

District of Columbia

Georgetown University	Washington

Georgia

Emory   University   Atlanta
Illinois
Lake Forest College   Lake Forest
Northwestern University   Evanston
University of Chicago   Chicago

Indiana
University of Notre Dame   Notre Dame
Wabash College   Crawfordsville

Iowa
Grinnell College   Grinnell

Maine
Bates College   Lewiston
Bowdoin College   Brunswick
Colby College   Waterville

Massachusetts
Amherst College   Amherst
Boston College   Chestnut Hill
College of the Holy Cross   Worcester
Harvard University   Cambridge
Massachusetts Institute   Cambridge
of Technology
Mount Holyoke College   South Hadley
Smith College   Northampton
Tufts University   Medford
Wellesley College   Wellesley
Williams College   Williamstown

Minnesota
Carleton College   Northfield
Macalester College   St. Paul
St. Olaf College   Northfield

Missouri
Washington University in St. Louis   St. Louis

New Hampshire
Dartmouth College   Hanover

New Jersey
Princeton University   Princeton

New York
Barnard College   New York
Colgate University   Hamilton
Columbia University, The Fu   New York
  Foundation School of Engineering
  and Applied Science
Cornell University   Ithaca
Hamilton College   Clinton
Union College   Schenectady
University of Rochester   Rochester
Vassar College   Poughkeepsie

North Carolina
Campbell University   Buies Creek
Davidson College   Davidson
Duke University   Durham
Salem College   Winston-Salem
University of North Carolina   Chapel Hill

Ohio
Oberlin College   Oberlin
Kenyon College   Gambier

Oregon
Reed College   Portland

Pennsylvania

Bryn Mawr College	Bryn Mawr
Bucknell University	Lewisburg
California University of Pennsylvania	California
Gettysburg College	Gettysburg
Haverford College	Haverford
Lafayette College	Lafayette
Swarthmore College	Swarthmore
University of Pennsylvania	Philadelphia

Rhode Island

Brown University	Providence

Tennessee

Vanderbilt University	Nashville

Texas

Rice University	Houston

Vermont

Middlebury College	Middlebury

Virginia

University of Richmond	Richmond
University of Virginia	Charlottesville
Washington and Lee University	Lexington

Wisconsin

Beloit College	Beloit
Lawrence University	Appleton

State Agencies

Alabama
Alabama Commission on Higher Education
Phone: 1-800-960-7773
Web site: www.ache.state.al.us

Alaska
Alaska Commission on Postsecondary Education
Toll-free: 1-800-441-2962
Web site: www.alaskaadvantage.state.ak.us

Arizona
Arizona Commission for Postsecondary Education
Phone: (602) 258-2435
Web site: www.azhighered.org

Arkansas
Arkansas Department of Higher Education
Toll-free: 1-800-54-STUDY
Web site: www.arkansashighered.com

California
California Student Aid Commission
Toll-free: 1-888-224-7268
Web site: www.csac.ca.gov

Colorado
Colorado Commission on Higher Education
Phone: (303) 866-2723
Web site: www.state.co.us/cche

Connecticut
Connecticut State Department of Education

Phone: (860) 947-1855
Web Site: www.ctdhe.org

Delaware
Delaware Higher Education Commission
Toll-free: 1-800-292-7935
Web site: www.doe.state.de.us/high-ed

District of Columbia
Office of the State Superintendent of Education
Phone: (202) 727-2824
Web site: www.seo.dc.gov

Florida
Office of Student Financial Assitance,
Florida Department of Education
Toll-free: 1-888-827-2004
Web site: www.floridastudentfinancialaid.org

Georgia
Georgia Student Finance Commission
Toll-Free: 1-800-505-4732
Web site: www.gsfc.org

Hawaii
University of Hawaii System
Phone: (808) 956-7251
Web site: www.hawaii.edu/admissions/aid.html

Idaho
Idaho State Board of Education
Phone: (208) 332-1574
Web site: www.boardofed.idaho.gov/scholarships

Illinois
Illinois Student Assistance Commission
Toll-free: 1-800-899-4722

Web site: www.collegezone.com

Indiana
State Student Assistance Commission of Indiana
Toll-free: 1-888-528-4719
Web site: www. in.gov/ssaci

Iowa
Iowa College Student Aid Commission
Toll-free: 1-877-272-4456
Phone: (515) 725-3400
Web site: www.iowacollegeaid.org

Kansas
Kansas Board of Regents
Phone: (785) 296-3421
Web site: www.kansasregents.org

Kentucky
Kentucky Higher Education Assistance Authority
Toll-free: 1-800-928-8926
Web site: www.kheaa.com

Louisiana
Louisiana Office of Student Financial Assistance
Toll-free: 1-800-259-5626
Web site: www.osfa.state.la.us

Maine
Finance Authority of Maine
Toll-free: 1-800-228-3734
Web site: www.famemaine.com

Maryland
Maryland Higher Education Commission
Toll-free: 1-800-974-1024
Web site: www.mhec.state.md.us

Massachusetts
Massachusetts Board of Higher Education, Office of Student
Financial Assistance
Phone: (617) 727-9420
Web Site: www.osfa.mass.edu

Michigan
Student financial Services Bureau
Toll-free: 1-800-642-5626, ext. 37054
Web site: www.michigan.gov/mistudentaid

Minnesota
Minnesota Office of Higher Education
Toll-free: 1-800-657-3866
Web site: www.ohe.state.mn.us

Mississippi
Mississippi Office of Student Financial Aid, Mississippi Institutions
of Higher Learning
Toll-free: 1-800-327-2980
Web site: www.mississippi.edu/riseupms/financialaid-state.php

Missouri
Missouri Department of Higher Education
Toll-free: 1-800-473-6757
Web site: www.dhe.mo.gov

Montana
Montana Guaranteed Student Loan Program
Toll-free: 1-800-537-7508
Web site: www.mgslp.state.mt.us

Nebraska
Nebraska Coordinating Commission for Postsecondary Education
Phone: (402) 471-2847
Web site: www.ccpe.state.ne.us

Nevada
Office of the State Treasurer
Toll-free: 1-888-477-2667
Web site: www.nevadatreasurer.gov

New Hampshire
New Hampshire Postsecondary Education Commission
Phone: (603) 271-2555
Web site: www.nh.gov/postsecondary/financial/index.html

New Jersey
New Jersey Higher Education Student Assistance Authority
Toll-free: 1-800-792-8670
Web site: www.hesaa.org

New Mexico
New Mexico Higher Education Department
Toll-free: 1-800-279-9777
Web site: www.hed.state.nm.us

New York
New York State Higher Education Services Corporation
Toll-free: 1-888-697-4372
Web site: www.hesc.org

North Carolina
College Foundation of North Carolina
Toll-free: 1-866-866-2362
Web site: www.cfnc.org

North Dakota
North Dakota University System
Phone: (701) 328-2960
Web site: www.ndus.edu

Ohio
Ohio Board of Regents
Toll-free: 1-888-833-1133
(for information specifically about Ohio programs)
Toll-free: 1-877-428-8246
(for information about other sources of financial aid)
Web site: www.regents.ohio.gov/sgs/index.php

Oklahoma
Oklahoma State Regents for Higher Education
Toll-free: 1-800-858-1840
Web site: www.okhighered.org

Oregon
Oregon Student Assistance Commission
Phone: (541) 687-7400
Toll-free: 1-800-452-8807
Web site: www.osac.state.or.us

Pennsylvania
Pennsylvania Higher Education Assistance Agency
Toll-free: 1-800-692-7392
Web site: www.pheaa.org

Rhode Island
Rhode Island Higher Education Assistance Authority
Toll-free: 1-800-922-9855
Web site: www.riheaa.org/borrowers

South Carolina
South Carolina Commission on Higher Education
Toll-free: 1-803-737-2260
Web site: www.che.sc.gov

South Dakota
South Dakota Board of Regents

Phone: (605) 773-3455
Web site: www.sdbor.ed/student/prospective

Tennessee
Tennessee Student Assistance Corporation
Toll-free: 1-800-342-1663
Web site: www.collegepaystn.com

Texas
Texas Higher Education Coordinating Board; Texas Financial Aid
Information Center
Toll-free: 1-888-311-8881
Web site: www.collegefortexans.com

Utah
Utah Higher Education Assistance Authority
Toll-free: 1-877-336-7378
Web site: www.uheaa.org

Vermont
Vermont Student Assistance Corporation
Toll-free: 1-800-642-3177
Web site: www.vsac.org

Virginia
State Council of Higher Education for Virginia
Toll-free: 1-877-516-0138
Web site: www.schev.edu

Washington
Washington State Higher Education Coordinating Board
Toll-free: 1-888-535-0747
Web site: www.hecb.wa.gov

West Virginia
West Virginia Higher Education Policy Commission
Toll-free: 1-888-825-5707

Web site: www.hepc.wvnet.edu

Wisconsin
Wisconsin Higher Education Aids Board
Phone: (608) 267-2206
Web site: www.heab.wisconsin.gov

Wyoming
Wyoming Department of Education
Phone: (307) 777-7690
Web site: www.k12.wy.us/grants.asp

GLOSSARY

Adjusted Gross Income: The sum of earned income, unearned income, and business income, less adjustments to income.

Award Letter: Letter from the school notifying the student of the types and amounts of financial aid being offered for the school year.

Award Year: The award year, for financial aid purposes, is from July 1st to June 30th.

Base-year Income: Income from the tax year preceding the Award Year.
(Example: 2011 income impacts 2012-13 financial aid.)

Campus-Based Aid: Financial aid programs funded by the Federal Government and administered directly by the financial aid office of each participating school. There are three primary campus-based aid programs: Federal Supplemental Educational Opportunity Grant (FSEOG), Federal Work-Study (FWS), and Federal Perkins Loan.

College Scholarship Services (CSS): The financial aid division of *The College Board*, processor for the Financial Aid *Profile* application.

Consolidation Loan: Either a Direct or FFEL loan that allows the borrower to combine different types and amounts of Federal loans to simplify repayment and pay off the existing loans.

Cost of Education (or Cost of Attendance): The total amount it will cost a student to go to school, usually expressed as a yearly figure. The cost of education covers tuition and fees, on-campus room and board (or a housing and food allowance for off-campus students), and allowances for books, supplies, transportation, childcare, costs related to a disability, and miscellaneous expenses.

Deadline: The date by which each individual school requires the FAFSA be completed and received by the processing center. The FAFSA cannot be mailed out until after January 1; most schools set deadlines early in the calendar year. If applying to schools with different deadlines, the forms should be mailed out prior to the earliest required date.

Default: Failure to repay a student loan according to the terms agreed to when the student signed a promissory note. Default also may result from failure to submit a request for deferment or cancellation on time.

Deferment: A postponement of repayment on a loan. During deferment, no payments are required but depending on the type of loan (subsidized, unsubsidized, PLUS) the borrower may still be responsible for the interest during the deferment period.

Dependent Student: A student who, for financial aid purposes, is classified as dependent on his/her parents for his/her primary support; when applying for financial aid, the parents' income and asset information will be reported along with the dependent student's.

Discharge: The release from all obligations of repayment of a loan due to certain circumstances, such as the total and permanent disability or death of the borrower.

Education Savings and Asset Protection Allowance: The amount of assets excluded from assessment in Federal Need Analysis.

Expected Family Contribution: An amount, determined by a formula established by Congress, that indicates how much of the family's financial resources should be available to help pay college costs.

Federal Aid: Student financial aid programs sponsored by the U.S. Department of Education which include Federal Pell Grants, Federal Supplemental Educational Opportunity Grants (FSEOG), Federal Work-Study (FWS), Federal Perkins Loans, Federal Direct Loans, and Federal PLUS Loans.

Federal Need Analysis Methodology: The formula, established by Congress, that calculates the family's Expected Family Contribution.

Federal Pell Grant: A grant awarded to undergraduates attending school at least halftime, on the basis of financial need.

Federal Perkins Loan: A low-interest loan (5%) for undergraduate and graduate students with exceptional financial need, as determined by the school.

Federal PLUS Loan: A loan for parents that enable them to borrow for each child who is enrolled at least half time and are a dependent student. The annual loan limit is the student's cost of education minus any financial aid received.

Federal Direct (Stafford) Loan: Low-interest loan made to undergraduate and graduate students attending school at least half time; may be subsidized or unsubsidized, depending on financial need.

Federal Supplemental Education Opportunity Grant (FSEOG): A grant awarded to undergraduates with exceptional financial need, as determined by the school, with priority given to Federal Pell Grant recipients.

Federal Work-Study (FWS): A program that provides jobs for undergraduate and graduate students who need financial aid. FWS provides the student the opportunity to earn money to help pay for educational expenses.

Financial Aid Administrator: A person employed by the college or university who is responsible for the administration and distribution of financial aid to its students.

Financial Aid Package: The total financial aid a student receives for a given award year. Federal, state, and institutional aid are combined into a package to help meet the student's financial need.

Financial Aid *Profile* Application: A customized financial aid form designed and processed by *College Scholarship Services*. It contains specific questions chosen by participating schools designed to qualify students for institutional aid. Unlike the Federal "Free Application," this form requires a processing fee for each school listed.

Financial Need: The difference between the student's cost of attendance and the Expected Family Contribution.

Forbearance: A period of time when loan repayments are postponed or reduced due to the borrower's inability to make scheduled payments.

Free Application for Federal Student Aid (FAFSA): The Federal application filled out by the student that collects household and financial information to be used to calculate the Expected Family Contribution. This application qualifies the student for Federal aid programs.

Gift Aid: Type of financial aid which the student does not have to repay; includes grants and scholarships.

Grace Period: The period of time before repayment of a student loan must begin. Depending on the type of loan, the student will have a grace period of six to nine months after he/she graduates, leaves school or drops below half-time.

Grant: Federal, state and/or institutional financial aid that the student does not have to repay- Gift Aid.

Half-time: At schools measuring progress by credit hours and academic terms (semesters, trimester, or quarters), half-time means at least 6 semester or quarter hours per term. At schools measuring progress by credit hours but not using academic terms, half time means at least 12 semester hours or 18-quarter hours per year. Individual schools may choose to set higher minimums than these.

Hope Scholarship Credit: A tax credit that may be claimed for qualified tuition and expenses for students enrolled at least half time in one of the first two years of postsecondary education.

Independent Student: A student who, for financial aid purposes, is classified as not having access to parental support and may exclude parent's income and assets when completing the financial aid forms. The criteria for determining independence for Federal, state and institutional aid may differ.

Institutional Aid: Student financial aid disseminated by the schools, usually in the form of grants and need-based scholarships.

Legal Guardian: An individual appointed by the courts to provide support for the student.

Lifetime Learning Tax Credit: A tax credit that may be claimed for qualified tuition and related expenses for students who are enrolled in eligible educational institutions.

Merit Aid: Financial aid awarded on the basis of the student's academic, athletic, and/or extracurricular excellence.

Need Analysis: The process of analyzing the household and financial information on the student's financial aid application and calculating an Expected Family Contribution.

Need-Based Aid: Financial aid awarded on the basis of the family's financial and personal situation.

Need Analysis Processing Center: An agency contracted by the Department of Education to process completed financial aid forms.

Origination Fee: A fee deducted from each disbursement of a Federal loan for processing and insurance costs.

Preparer: An individual, other than the student, student's spouse, or student's parent, who completes the Free Application for Federal Student Aid. The law requires that such an individual complete and sign the Preparer section of the FAFSA, even if he/she is not paid for his/her services.

Professional Judgment: The ability of a school's Financial Aid Administrator to make adjustments in the Formula used to calculate the Expected Family Contribution due to "special conditions," for example, excessive medical expenses, or to override a student's dependency status. Adjustments are made on a case-by-case basis.

Promissory Note: The binding legal documents signed when the student gets a student loan. It lists the conditions under which the student is borrowing and the terms of repayment. It also includes information regarding the interest, deferment, and cancellation provisions.

ROTC: The Reserve Officers' Training Corps prepares college students for officer leadership positions in the Army, Navy, Air Force and Marine Corps. Normally, ROTC participants take one military science course along with their other college courses. Upon graduation, you become a commissioned officer.

Self-help: Type of financial aid that the student must either repay or work for (loans and Work-Study).

Special Conditions: Special circumstances, such as excessive medical expenses, elementary or secondary private school tuition, loss of job, death, or divorce, which would impact the parent's ability to pay college costs. In such a situation, the Financial Aid Administrator may use "professional judgment" to adjust the Expected Family Contribution.

Student Aid Report (SAR): The document printed by the need-analysis processing center, which contains the financial and other information reported on the Free Application for Federal Student Aid. This report is mailed to the student approximately four weeks after submission of the FAFSA, and indicates the student's Expected Family Contribution and Pell Grant eligibility.

Unearned Income: Taxable income which includes interest, dividends and capital gains.

Untaxed Income: Income which is not taxed but must be reported on the financial aid forms and includes deductible IRA's, Keogh's, tax-sheltered annuities, 401k plans, workers compensation, untaxed disability payments and tax-exempt interest.

Verification: The process of checking the accuracy of the information entered on the financial aid form. Verification is administered by the college that the student is or will be attending.